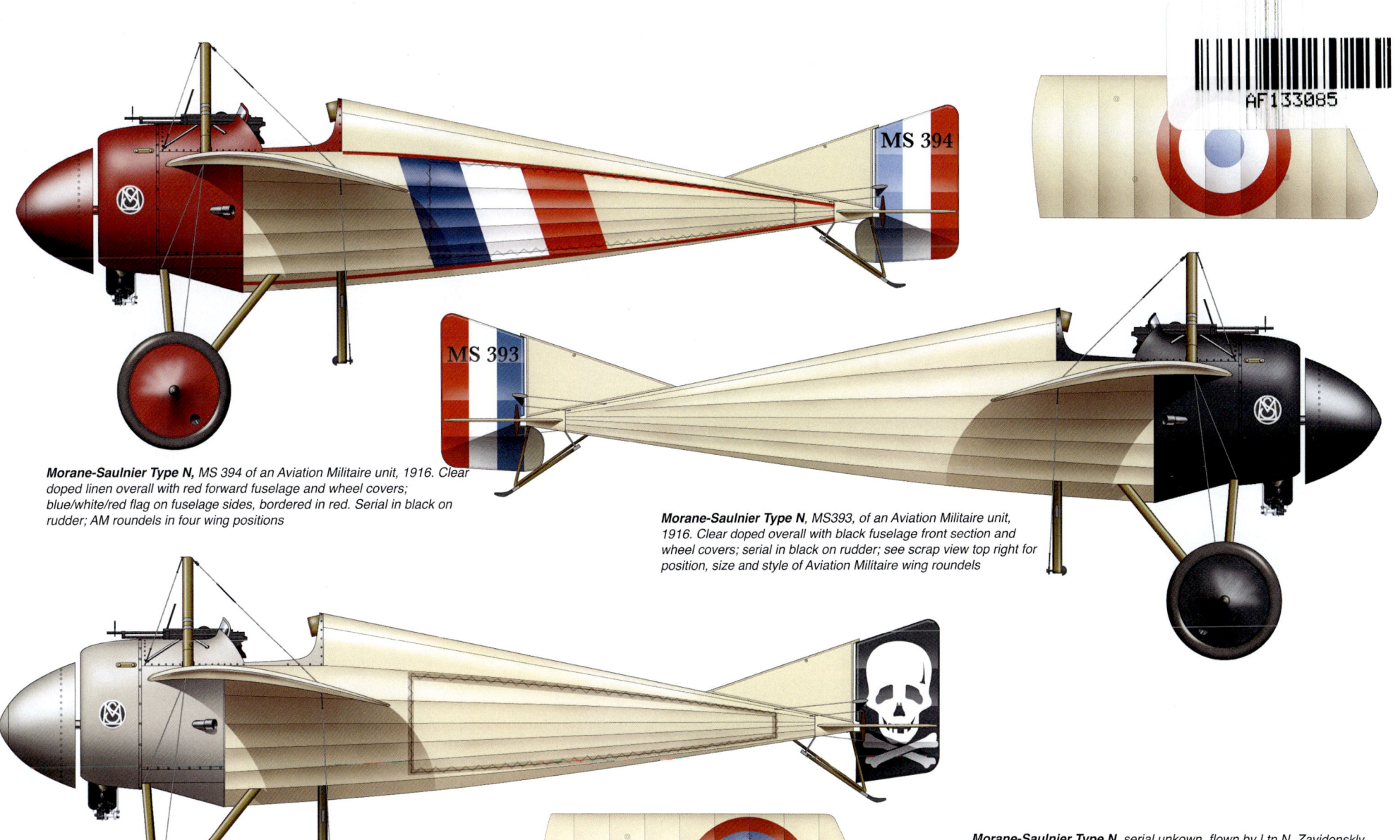

Morane-Saulnier Type N, MS 394 of an Aviation Militaire unit, 1916. Clear doped linen overall with red forward fuselage and wheel covers; blue/white/red flag on fuselage sides, bordered in red. Serial in black on rudder; AM roundels in four wing positions

Morane-Saulnier Type N, MS393, of an Aviation Militaire unit, 1916. Clear doped overall with black fuselage front section and wheel covers; serial in black on rudder; see scrap view top right for position, size and style of Aviation Militaire wing roundels

Morane-Saulnier Type N, serial unkown, flown by Ltn N. Zavidonskly, 11th CAS, Imperial Russian Air Service, 1916. Doped linen overall with front section and wheel covers in brown. Black rudder with white skull and cross-bones. IRAS roundels in four wing positions. Zavidonskly scored one victory flying this aircraft; see scrap view below left for position, size and style of Imperial Russian Air Service wing roundels

America Joins In

When World War I erupted in 1914, American President Woodrow Wilson declared the United States as a neutral country, a stance approved by the majority of the population. The war of attrition that Germany had adopted against all shipping in war zones left numerous victims among American vessels, an affair that by early 1917 had angered Wilson enough to break diplomatic relations with Germany. Congress granted the US President's request for a decleration of war on 6 April.

Less than two months later the first US troops landed in France, marking an end to a three-year stalemate in the bloodied fighting from both sides. However, years of stagnation in aeroplane development and a near complete neglect to the setting up of a proper air arm meant that the US entered the war completely unprepared. The only source of flying material for the American Expeditionary Force was France, and probably the most significant aeroplane to be operated by American aviators during World War I was the Nieuport 28.

This small, agile fighting machine was soon to become the mount of some of the most famous pilots, and a shining star above all others was Captain Eddie Rickenbacher, often called America's Ace of Aces.

Edward Vernon Rickenbacher was born in Columbus (Ohio), on 8 October 1890 of Swiss immigrants, the third of eight children. He graduated after only 187 days as student pilot and was comissioned Lieutenant and assigned to the 94th Aero Squadron under the command of Major John Huffer. He was coached in aerial tactics by Major Raoul Lufbery at the unit's base of Gengoult Aerodrome (Toul). On 29 April 1918 he shared his first victory with Captain James Norman Hall and on 7 May he scored his first solo victory.

He made headlines in the US press when he became an 'ace' and by 30 May he scored his sixth victory with a seventh chalked up on 14 September (a Fokker D.VII), after having being absent through some weeks in July due to an abscess in his ear that needed treatment.

Rickenbacher was given command of the 94th Aero on 25 September 1918. That same day he earned the French Croix de Guerre for taking single-handed a flight of five Fokkers and two Halberstadt CL.IIs, shooting down one of each; he was also awarded the US Medal of Honor for the same action, only it arrived 12 years later. His tally stood at 12 in October, and by that time he was flying SPAD 13s with which the unit started to be supplied around mid-July. He finished the war with 26 claimed victories though these were later reduced to 24.33.

The Nieuport 28 C.1
Built by the Société Anonyme des Éstablissements Nieuport, the 28 C.1 was a single-seat single-engined biplane fighter designed and built for the French air force. It was however rejected in favour of the SPAD S.XIII. With no American fighter aircraft available, the US Air Service acquired 297 Nieuport 28s for the American Expeditionary Force and assigned to the 94th and 95th Aero Squadrons. As these two units converted to the SPAD, their surviving aircraft were handed over to the new arrivals, the 27th and 147th Aero Squadrons. By the end of August all four squadrons were equipped with SPADs.

During the intensive military operations it was discovered that the wing canvas could be torn off during extreme manouvres and while Nieuport eventually solved this problem the American units had already converted onto the SPAD. The new mount of the Aero Squadrons was studier though less nimble in the air their previous equipment.

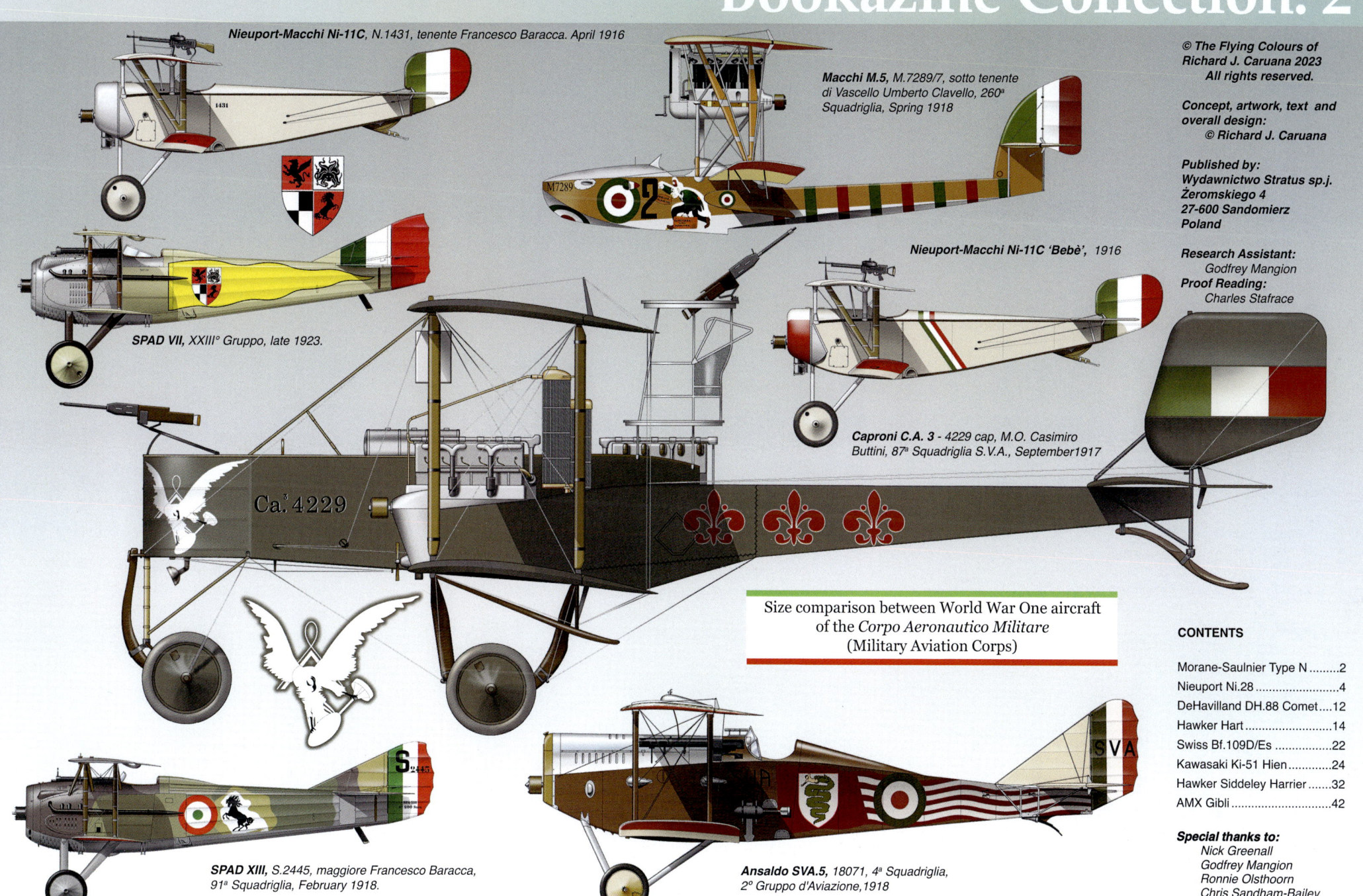

Morane-Saulnier Type N

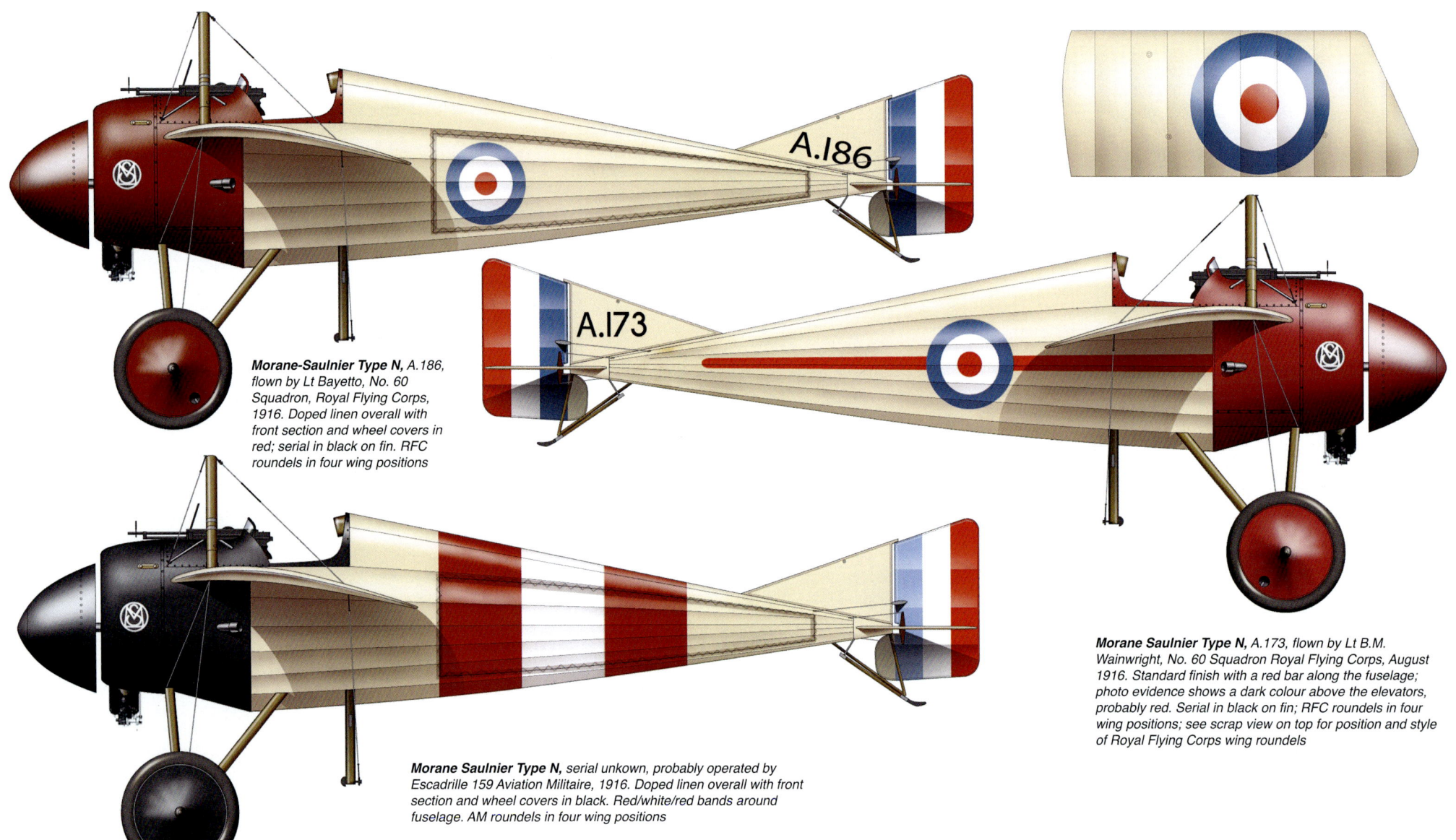

Morane-Saulnier Type N, A.186, flown by Lt Bayetto, No. 60 Squadron, Royal Flying Corps, 1916. Doped linen overall with front section and wheel covers in red; serial in black on fin. RFC roundels in four wing positions

Morane Saulnier Type N, serial unkown, probably operated by Escadrille 159 Aviation Militaire, 1916. Doped linen overall with front section and wheel covers in black. Red/white/red bands around fuselage. AM roundels in four wing positions

Morane Saulnier Type N, A.173, flown by Lt B.M. Wainwright, No. 60 Squadron Royal Flying Corps, August 1916. Standard finish with a red bar along the fuselage; photo evidence shows a dark colour above the elevators, probably red. Serial in black on fin; RFC roundels in four wing positions; see scrap view on top for position and style of Royal Flying Corps wing roundels

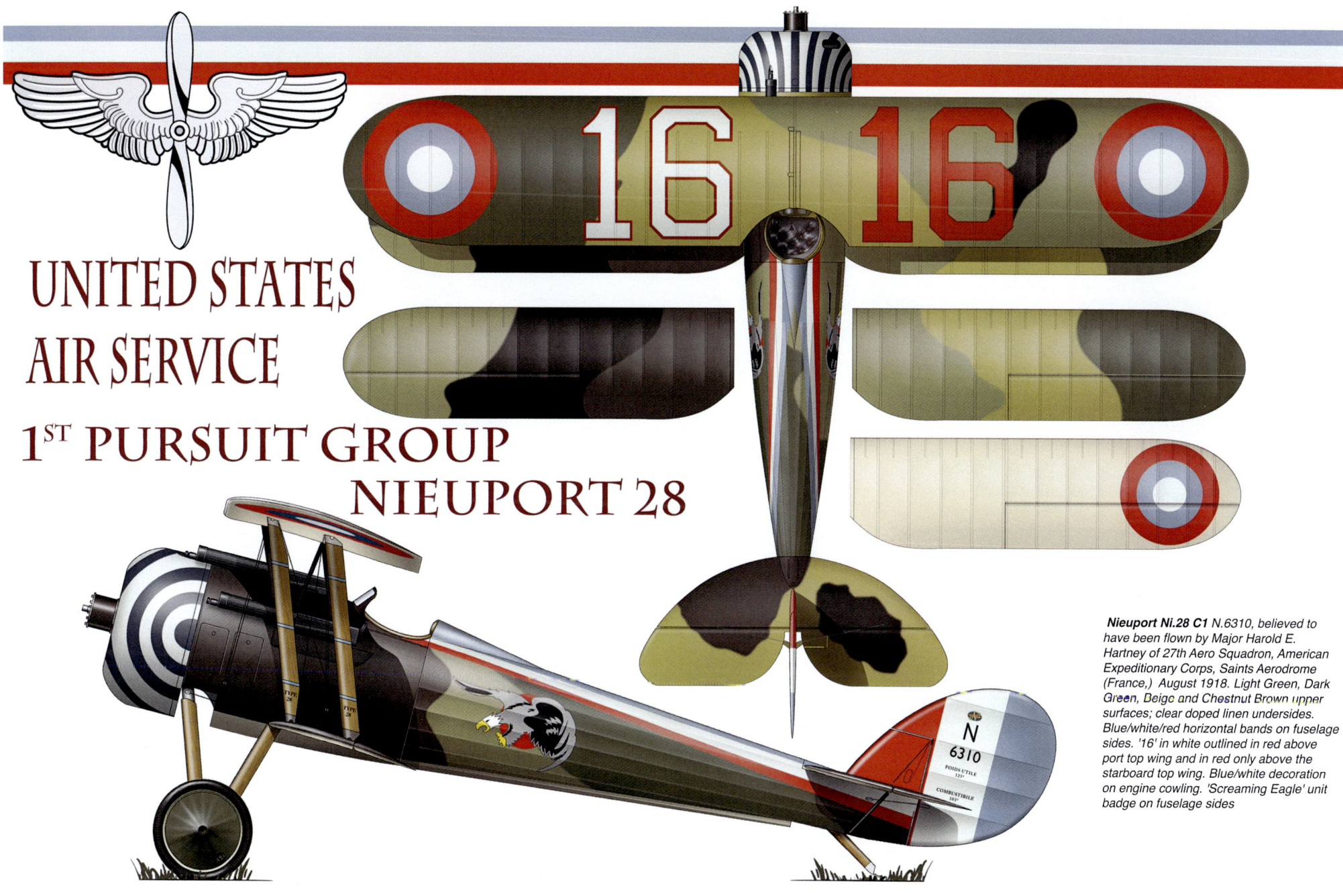

UNITED STATES AIR SERVICE
1ST PURSUIT GROUP
NIEUPORT 28

Nieuport Ni.28 C1 N.6310, believed to have been flown by Major Harold E. Hartney of 27th Aero Squadron, American Expeditionary Corps, Saints Aerodrome (France,) August 1918. Light Green, Dark Green, Beige and Chestnut Brown upper surfaces; clear doped linen undersides. Blue/white/red horizontal bands on fuselage sides. '16' in white outlined in red above port top wing and in red only above the starboard top wing. Blue/white decoration on engine cowling. 'Screaming Eagle' unit badge on fuselage sides

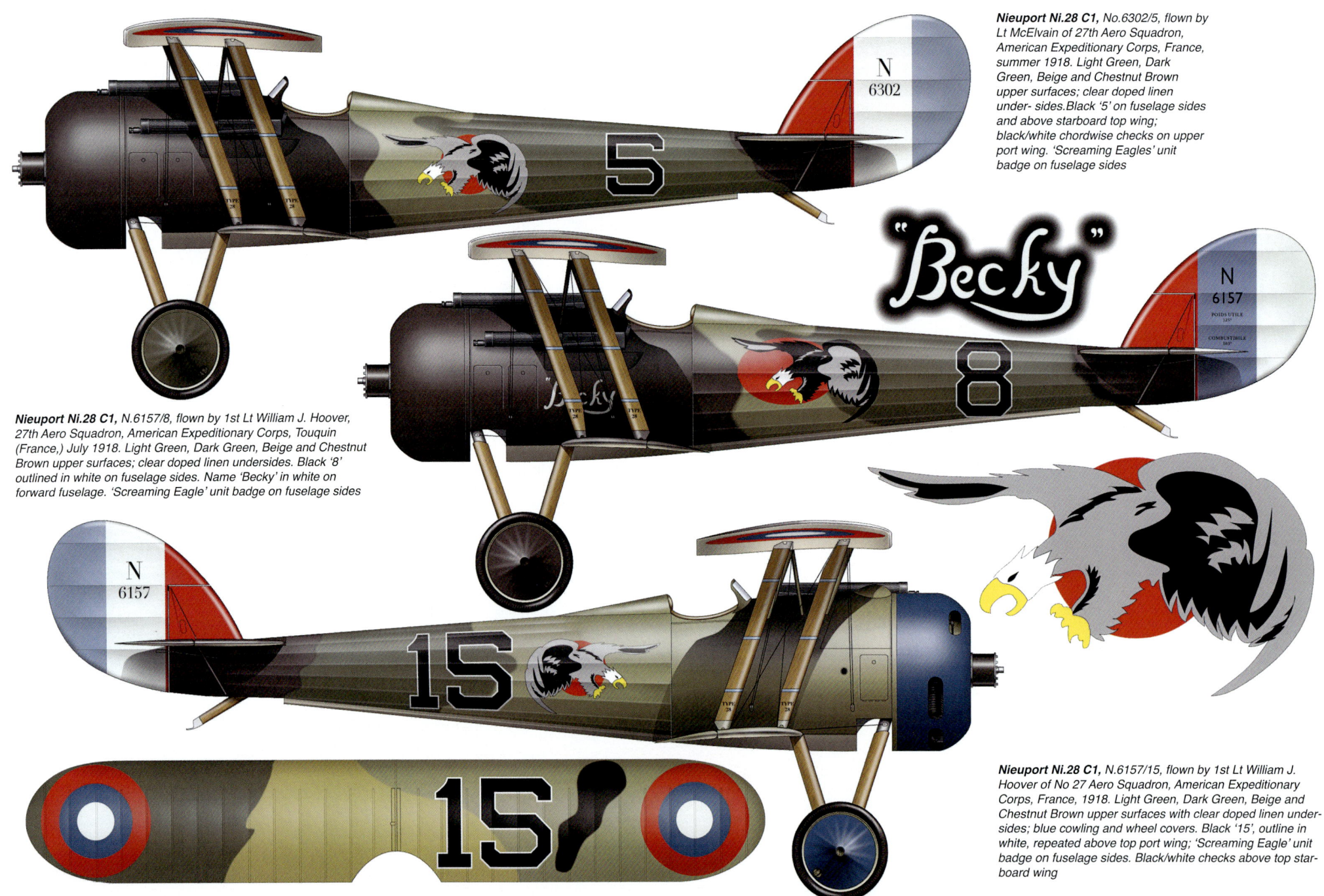

Nieuport Ni.28 C1, No.6302/5, flown by Lt McElvain of 27th Aero Squadron, American Expeditionary Corps, France, summer 1918. Light Green, Dark Green, Beige and Chestnut Brown upper surfaces; clear doped linen under- sides. Black '5' on fuselage sides and above starboard top wing; black/white chordwise checks on upper port wing. 'Screaming Eagles' unit badge on fuselage sides

Nieuport Ni.28 C1, N.6157/8, flown by 1st Lt William J. Hoover, 27th Aero Squadron, American Expeditionary Corps, Touquin (France,) July 1918. Light Green, Dark Green, Beige and Chestnut Brown upper surfaces; clear doped linen undersides. Black '8' outlined in white on fuselage sides. Name 'Becky' in white on forward fuselage. 'Screaming Eagle' unit badge on fuselage sides

Nieuport Ni.28 C1, N.6157/15, flown by 1st Lt William J. Hoover of No 27 Aero Squadron, American Expeditionary Corps, France, 1918. Light Green, Dark Green, Beige and Chestnut Brown upper surfaces with clear doped linen undersides; blue cowling and wheel covers. Black '15', outline in white, repeated above top port wing; 'Screaming Eagle' unit badge on fuselage sides. Black/white checks above top starboard wing

Nieuport Ni.28 C.1, N.6169, flown by 1st Lt Edwar V. Rickenbacker of 94th Aero Squadron, American Expeditionary Corps, France, 1918. Light Green, Dark Green, Beige and Chestnut Brown upper surfaces with clear doped linen undersides; white/red/blue cowl- ing. White '1' with blue and red drop shadows; 'Hat in Ring' unit badge on both fuselage sides. The pilot flew this aircraft when he scored his third victory on 17 May, and also those of 22, 28 and 30 May 1918

Above and Scrap Top Right: Nieuport Ni.28 C1, N6159/12, flown by 1st Lt Edward V. Rickenbacker, 94th Aero Squadron American Aero Expeditionary Force, France, June 1918. Light Green, Dark Green, Beige and Chestnut Brown upper surfaces with clear doped linen undersides. White engine cowling; white '12' with red outline. 'Hat in Ring' unit badge on fuselage sides. 'Liberty Bonds' posters applied to the upper and lower wing surfaces

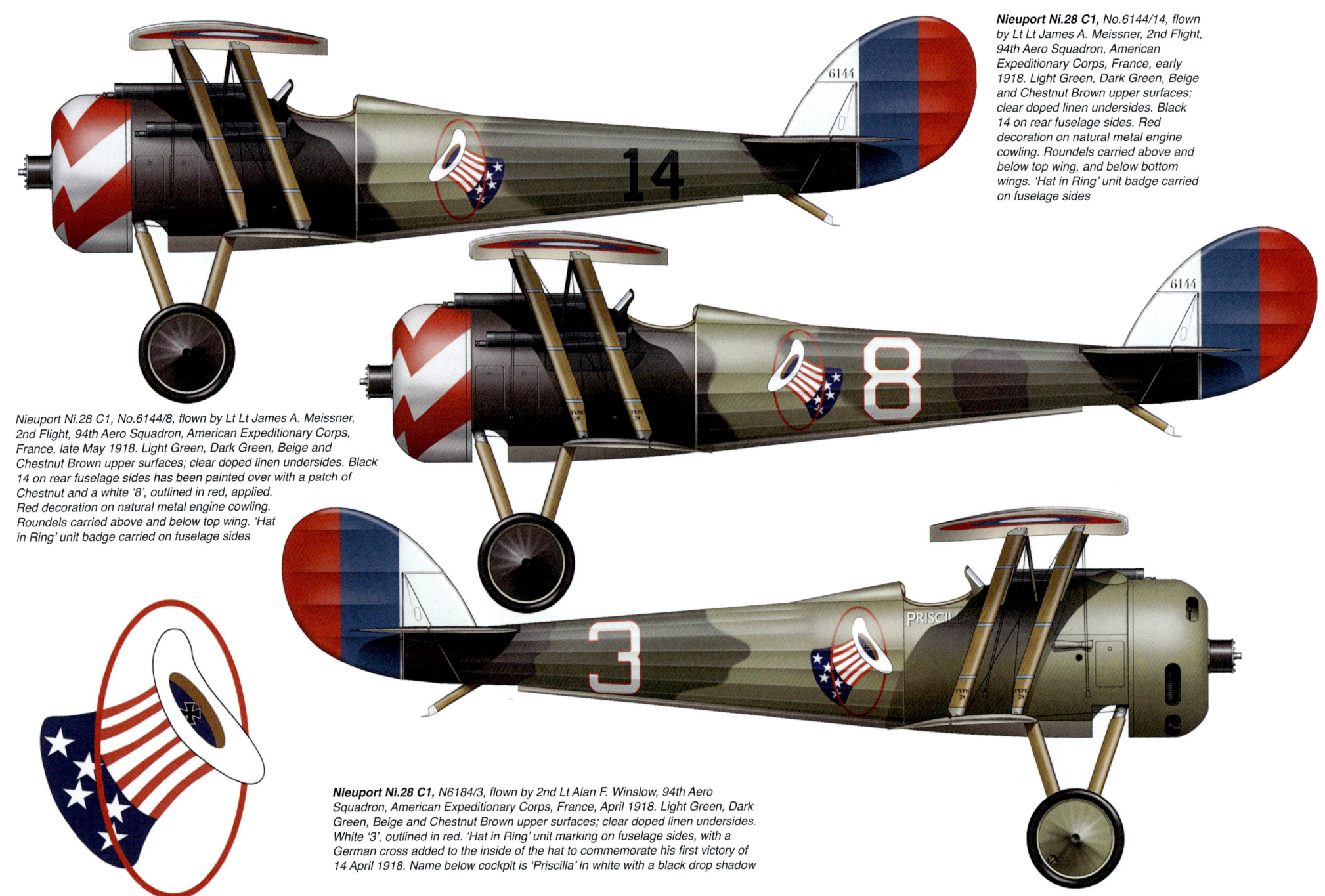

Nieuport Ni.28 C1, No.6144/14, flown by Lt Lt James A. Meissner, 2nd Flight, 94th Aero Squadron, American Expeditionary Corps, France, early 1918. Light Green, Dark Green, Beige and Chestnut Brown upper surfaces; clear doped linen undersides. Black 14 on rear fuselage sides. Red decoration on natural metal engine cowling. Roundels carried above and below top wing, and below bottom wings. 'Hat in Ring' unit badge carried on fuselage sides

Nieuport Ni.28 C1, No.6144/8, flown by Lt Lt James A. Meissner, 2nd Flight, 94th Aero Squadron, American Expeditionary Corps, France, late May 1918. Light Green, Dark Green, Beige and Chestnut Brown upper surfaces; clear doped linen undersides. Black 14 on rear fuselage sides has been painted over with a patch of Chestnut and a white '8', outlined in red, applied. Red decoration on natural metal engine cowling. Roundels carried above and below top wing. 'Hat in Ring' unit badge carried on fuselage sides

Nieuport Ni.28 C1, N6184/3, flown by 2nd Lt Alan F. Winslow, 94th Aero Squadron, American Expeditionary Corps, France, April 1918. Light Green, Dark Green, Beige and Chestnut Brown upper surfaces; clear doped linen undersides. White '3', outlined in red. 'Hat in Ring' unit marking on fuselage sides, with a German cross added to the inside of the hat to commemorate his first victory of 14 April 1918. Name below cockpit is 'Priscilla' in white with a black drop shadow

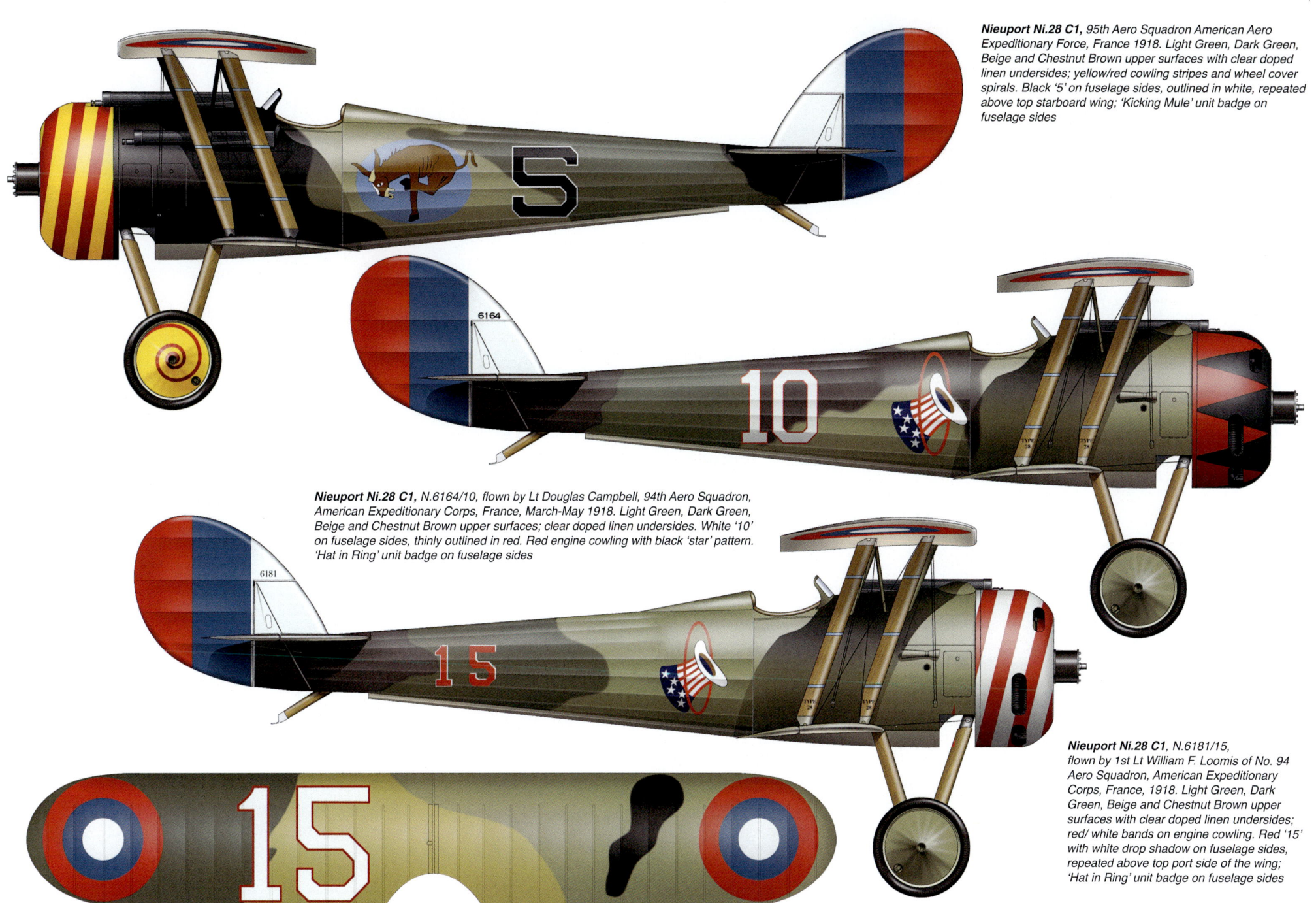

Nieuport Ni.28 C1, 95th Aero Squadron American Aero Expeditionary Force, France 1918. Light Green, Dark Green, Beige and Chestnut Brown upper surfaces with clear doped linen undersides; yellow/red cowling stripes and wheel cover spirals. Black '5' on fuselage sides, outlined in white, repeated above top starboard wing; 'Kicking Mule' unit badge on fuselage sides

Nieuport Ni.28 C1, N.6164/10, flown by Lt Douglas Campbell, 94th Aero Squadron, American Expeditionary Corps, France, March-May 1918. Light Green, Dark Green, Beige and Chestnut Brown upper surfaces; clear doped linen undersides. White '10' on fuselage sides, thinly outlined in red. Red engine cowling with black 'star' pattern. 'Hat in Ring' unit badge on fuselage sides

Nieuport Ni.28 C1, N.6181/15, flown by 1st Lt William F. Loomis of No. 94 Aero Squadron, American Expeditionary Corps, France, 1918. Light Green, Dark Green, Beige and Chestnut Brown upper surfaces with clear doped linen undersides; red/white bands on engine cowling. Red '15' with white drop shadow on fuselage sides, repeated above top port side of the wing; 'Hat in Ring' unit badge on fuselage sides

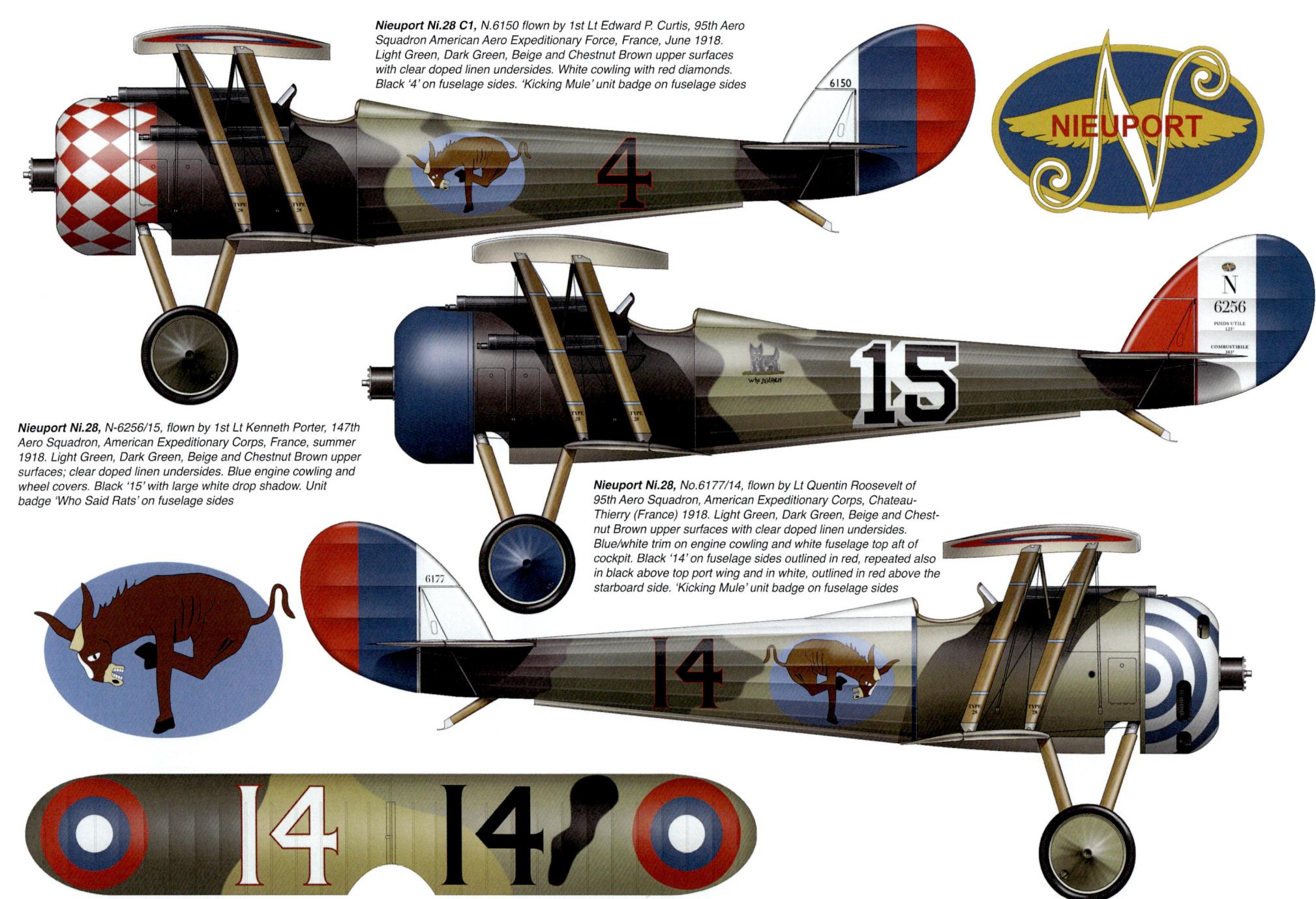

Nieuport Ni.28 C1, N.6150 flown by 1st Lt Edward P. Curtis, 95th Aero Squadron American Aero Expeditionary Force, France, June 1918. Light Green, Dark Green, Beige and Chestnut Brown upper surfaces with clear doped linen undersides. White cowling with red diamonds. Black '4' on fuselage sides. 'Kicking Mule' unit badge on fuselage sides

Nieuport Ni.28, N-6256/15, flown by 1st Lt Kenneth Porter, 147th Aero Squadron, American Expeditionary Corps, France, summer 1918. Light Green, Dark Green, Beige and Chestnut Brown upper surfaces; clear doped linen undersides. Blue engine cowling and wheel covers. Black '15' with large white drop shadow. Unit badge 'Who Said Rats' on fuselage sides

Nieuport Ni.28, No.6177/14, flown by Lt Quentin Roosevelt of 95th Aero Squadron, American Expeditionary Corps, Chateau-Thierry (France) 1918. Light Green, Dark Green, Beige and Chestnut Brown upper surfaces with clear doped linen undersides. Blue/white trim on engine cowling and white fuselage top aft of cockpit. Black '14' on fuselage sides outlined in red, repeated also in black above top port wing and in white, outlined in red above the starboard side. 'Kicking Mule' unit badge on fuselage sides

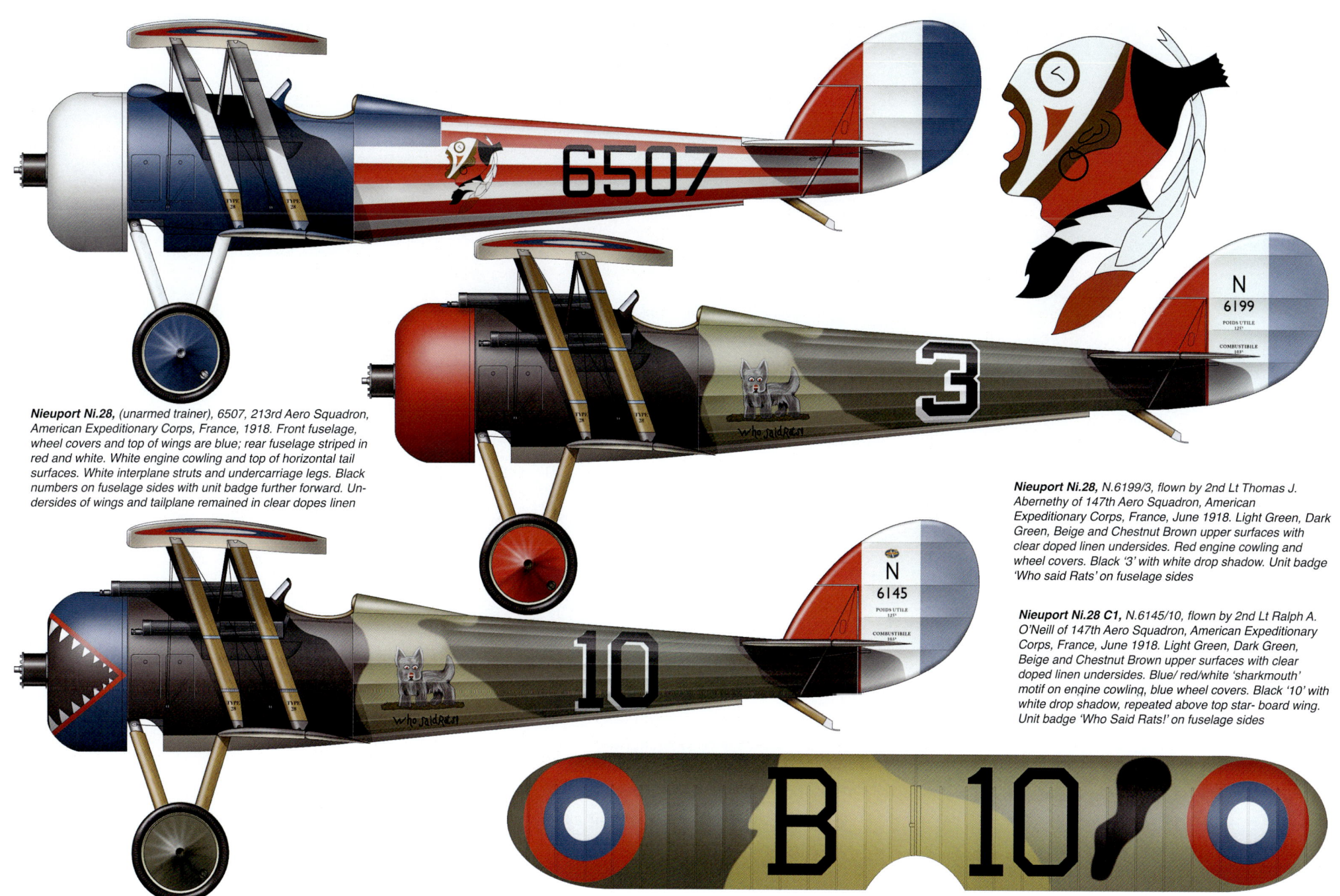

Nieuport Ni.28, (unarmed trainer), 6507, 213rd Aero Squadron, American Expeditionary Corps, France, 1918. Front fuselage, wheel covers and top of wings are blue; rear fuselage striped in red and white. White engine cowling and top of horizontal tail surfaces. White interplane struts and undercarriage legs. Black numbers on fuselage sides with unit badge further forward. Undersides of wings and tailplane remained in clear dopes linen

Nieuport Ni.28, N.6199/3, flown by 2nd Lt Thomas J. Abernethy of 147th Aero Squadron, American Expeditionary Corps, France, June 1918. Light Green, Dark Green, Beige and Chestnut Brown upper surfaces with clear doped linen undersides. Red engine cowling and wheel covers. Black '3' with white drop shadow. Unit badge 'Who said Rats' on fuselage sides

Nieuport Ni.28 C1, N.6145/10, flown by 2nd Lt Ralph A. O'Neill of 147th Aero Squadron, American Expeditionary Corps, France, June 1918. Light Green, Dark Green, Beige and Chestnut Brown upper surfaces with clear doped linen undersides. Blue/ red/white 'sharkmouth' motif on engine cowling, blue wheel covers. Black '10' with white drop shadow, repeated above top star- board wing. Unit badge 'Who Said Rats!' on fuselage sides

Those Magnificent Men...

Air races became popular soon after man learned to fly in heavier than air machines and no wonder that even the cinema celebrated such events with numerous movies; the one that readily comes to mind is 'Those Magnificent Men and Their Flying Machines'. From flights of fancy, to reality, and the epic 1934 MacRobertson Centenary Air Race from Mildenhall to Melbourne to commemorate the 100 years since the foundation of the Australian city. Sir Macpheroson Robertson, who had established his confectionary company in Fitzroy (Melbourne) in 1880 provided a prize pool of £15,000.

Divided into separate speed and handicap sections, the event attracted 64 entrants from 13 countries. However by the start of the race on 20 October 1934 these went down to 20 aircraft from seven countries. While some of the contestants picked readily available aircraft, De Havilland decided to design a special twin-engined racer to ensure that the British entry would continue to achieve the same prestige it garnered in the Schneider Trophy races.

With an estimated cost of £50,000 per aircraft De Havilland realised that it would have to part-sponsor and finance the project as a private venture, selling at a unit cost of £5,000. The first order received was for G-ACSP in February 1934. It was finished and flown for the first time on 8 September, a mere six weeks before the start of the race.

Design of the racer was assigned to Arthur Hagg who based his concept on a lightweight airframe of wooden construction except for load bearing components which were made of metal. It was powered by two 230hp Gipsy Six R engines driving two-bladed propellers that could automatically change pitch from fine to coarse as speed increased. A two-man crew sat in tandem under a framed canopy that hinged open to starboard. Main undercarriage wheels retracted into the engine cowlings while the tail was fitted with a skid.

Fuel capacity was provided for a range of nearly 4,800km to cover the distances between the five compulsory stops (Baghdad, Allahabad, Singapore, Darwin and Charleville) that stretched over nineteen countries and seven seas.

Three D.H. 88 'Comets' and their crews presented themselves at the start of the race, these being G-ASCP 'Black Magic' (race number 63), G-ACSR (race number 19) and G-ACSS 'Grosvenor House' (race number 34).

Top: De Havilland D.H. 88 Comet, *G-ACSS 'Grosvenor House', flown by C.W.A. Scott and Tom Campbell Black in the London to Melbourne race of 1934, winning the speed contest*

Above: De Havilland D.H. 88 Comet, *G-ACSP 'Black Magic' piloted by Jim and Amy Mollison in the London - Melbourne race, 1934. Sold to the Portuguese Government becoming CS-AAJ 'Salazar'. Rediscovered in the mid-1980s in Portugal and returned to the UK for reconstruction by Airspeed Aviation Ltd*

De Havilland D.H. 88 Comet, *G-ACSR, flown by Owen Cathcart-Jones and Ken Waller in the London-Melbourne race, 1934. Sold to the French Government the following year becoming F-ANPY 'Reine Astrid'*

The race started on 20 October 1934 from RAF Mildenhall with the winner of the speed division being C.W.A. Scott and T. Cambell Black in G-ACSS 'Grosvenor House', covering the distance in just under three days with 70 hours and 54 minutes of air time.

Winner of the handicap division with the second fastest time was the Dutch crew consisting of Parmentier, Moll, Prins and Van Brugge in the Douglas DC.2 named 'Uiver' (Stork), entered by KLM Airlines. Total air time was 81 hours and 10 minutes. There was only one Australian entry, a D.H. 80A Puss Moth named 'My Hildegarde', taking its pilot C.J. Melrose 120 hours to reach Melbourne to take second place in the handicap section.

Of the other two Comets, G-ACSP suffered a seized piston due to contaminated fuel and had to be retired while G-ACSR came in fourth in the race and flew back to England making the round trip in just over thirteen days.

Soon after, G-ACSS was taken over by the Air Ministry and serialled K-5084 until it suffered a heavy landing and was sold off for scrap. It was rebuilt and renamed 'The Burberry' carrying out a long distance flight from Gravesend to New Zealand and back, a total of 42,712km in 10 days, 21 hours and 22 minutes.

D.H. 88 Comet G-ACSS 'Grosvenor House' was rebuilt by De Havilland apprentices and was later brought to flying condition at the Shuttleworth Trust, Old Warden airfield, where it continues to thrill the crowds up to this very day

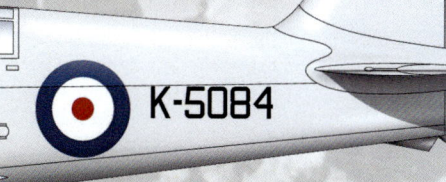

De Havilland DH 88 Comet, Grosvenor House G-ACSS, winner of the London to Melbourne air race, being inspected by a crowd of well wishers on its arrival (National Library of Australia)

Above: De Havilland D.H. 88 Comet, G-ACSS after it was acquired by the Air Ministry and serialled K-5084. It crashed twice during tests at Martlesham Heath and was sold for scrap, but was bought by F.E. Tasker and raced to fourth place in the 1937 Marseilles-Damascus-Paris race as G-ACSS 'The Orphan'

Left: De Havilland D.H. 88 Comet, G-ACSR after having been sold to the French Government in 1935, becoming F-ANPY 'Reine Astrid'. Generally used for record flights to French colonies until lost in a fire in 1940

De Havilland D.H.88 Comet, G-ADEF 'Boomerang', 1935. Silver overall with two-tone blue trim to fuselage and engine cowlings. Registration in dark blue on fuselage sides, above and below wings. 'Castrol' logo on top of rudder. Fifth and last Comet built for the King's Cup Air Race of September 1935 but did not take part. Crashed at Sudan in an attempt to fly London-Cape Town on 22 September 1935 flown by Cyril A. Nicholson and J.C. McArthur; no casualties

An Affair of the Hart

Reflecting on the situation within the British aviation industry during the immediate post-World War One era, one cannot fail to notice the apathy and economic instability that officialdom posed on aircraft development. Reliance on wartime aircraft had been stretched to the limit, and even beyond obsolescence in some cases while the aero-engine industry was practically in hibernation. Although designers were eager to explore and develop new techniques, new aircraft designs and better engines, finance for such projects was not available.

Operating with the meagre budgets on offer, Sydney Camm of H.G. Hawker Engineering Co. slowly progressed through a series of interesting and innovative projects such as the Hornbill and Heron of 1925. Of these, the former was of particular importance as the designer had built the smallest possible airframe around a powerful water-cooled in-line engine. Though the Heron was powered by the more conventional Jupiter radial, it introduced a metal fuselage primary structure developed by F. Sigrist, director-colleague of Sir Thomas Sopwith.

Through these and other fighter projects, Camm's conviction regarding the future of the water-cooled in-line engine gained ground and in 1926 he sought the assistance of Rolls-Royce whilst working on Air Ministry Specification 12/26 calling for a light bomber. It is important to mention here that this specification required the new aircraft to enter service in 1930. The timing was more dependent on the British Treasury's Ten Year Rule rather than foresight or the Royal Air Force's (RAF) service requirements.

Rolls-Royce responded by developing its Falcon F.I into the F.XIA, differing principally in having one-piece cast cylinder banks. On its part, Hawker progressed with its project under great secrecy, such was the cut-throat competition during that era. Through its two years of design development and prototype construction, Camm ensured that every sensible innovation that could be introduced into his design would be seriously considered, evaluated, tested and installed if found to be advantageous. Finally, J9052 was ready for its first

The first production Hart, J9933, that went through a series of developments during its life. In October 1930 it was re-engined with a Kestrel II to serve as Demon prototype Eventually J9933 went to No. 33 Squadron in September 1932, and later served also with No. 18 (Hawker Siddeley Aviation)

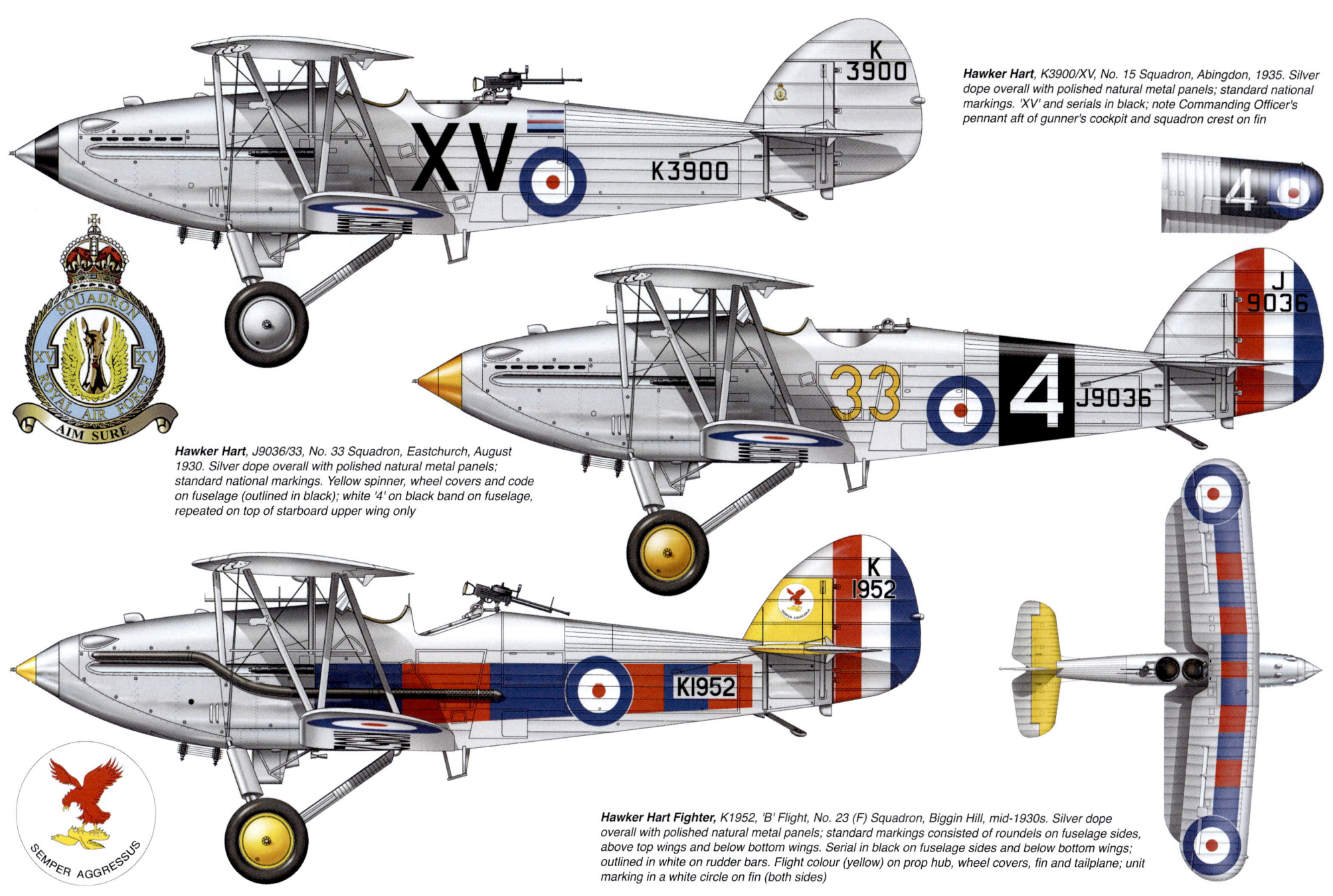

Hawker Hart, K3900/XV, No. 15 Squadron, Abingdon, 1935. Silver dope overall with polished natural metal panels; standard national markings. 'XV' and serials in black; note Commanding Officer's pennant aft of gunner's cockpit and squadron crest on fin

Hawker Hart, J9036/33, No. 33 Squadron, Eastchurch, August 1930. Silver dope overall with polished natural metal panels; standard national markings. Yellow spinner, wheel covers and code on fuselage (outlined in black); white '4' on black band on fuselage, repeated on top of starboard upper wing only

Hawker Hart Fighter, K1952, 'B' Flight, No. 23 (F) Squadron, Biggin Hill, mid-1930s. Silver dope overall with polished natural metal panels; standard markings consisted of roundels on fuselage sides, above top wings and below bottom wings. Serial in black on fuselage sides and below bottom wings; outlined in white on rudder bars. Flight colour (yellow) on prop hub, wheel covers, fin and tailplane; unit marking in a white circle on fin (both sides)

flight by Flt Lt P.W.S. 'George' Bulman in June 1928, followed by a six-month trial period at the Aeroplane and Armament Experimental Establishment (A&AEE) at Martlesham Heath. These, too, were conducted under a veil of strict security as it was not until a year later that Hawker's light bomber was publicly displayed at the Olympia Aero Show alongside the Hawker Hornet fighter and Tomtit trainer.

During competitive trials, the Hart (as it was now officially named) not only confirmed its superiority over the Fairey Fox II (J9834) and Avro Antelope (J9183) which were being offered under the same specification, but also put into obsolescence any fighter aircraft the RAF had on its inventory! It was clear that Hawker's light bomber heralded a new era in technical standards that paved the way for future projects. An initial production order for 15 development aircraft (J9933-J9947) was issued under Specification 9/29

In Service and Further Development
Twelve of the initial fifteen Harts on order were delivered in April 1930 to No. 33 Squadron, commanded by Sqn Ldr J.J. Breen, at Eastchurch, previously equipped with the Hawker Horsley. Well before the squadron had completed its work up period it placed second in the annual inter-unit bombing competition, barely three months from receiving its first Hart. One of the production development Harts was shipped to India where it was evaluated at Risalpur in an attempt to find a decent replacement to the Bristol Fighter and Siskin then in service. This aircraft was lost in an unfortunate bird-strike accident but enough testing had been carried out for the development and production of the Hart (India). Nos. 11, 39 and 60 Squadrons shared between them the 57 examples built of this type (K2083-K2132, K3921, K3922, K8627-K8631) to Specifications 9/31 and 12/33.

Further orders for Home Service squadrons had meanwhile also been placed, 82 examples being raised between 1930 and 1931. These consisted of 32 Hart I Bombers (K1416-K1447) to Contract No. 262750/30 and 50 Hart I Bombers and Hart C (communications) aircraft (K2424-K2473) under Contract No. 117876/31. Most of these went to re-equip a number of front-line bomber squadrons, including No. 12, 18 and 57.

The 1930 Air Exercises had proved the Hart to be superior not only to the RAF's contemporary bombers but also to all of its fighters, setting the phrase that 'it takes a Hart to catch a Hart'. While already well into its production phase, the Air Ministry issued Specification 15/30 calling for a fighter version to be powered by the Kestrel IIS. Hawker built six examples (K1950-K1955 to Contract No. 563380/30) which went to form a Flight within No. 23 Squadron based at Kenley. This version of the Hart formed the basis of the future Hawker Demon.

So radical was the Hart as a service machine that the need arose for a dual-control, training version. Such a modification was indeed simple, thanks to its original two-seat layout, although in actual fact the prototype (K1996) was converted from a Hawker Audax. A problem arose as the centre of gravity shifted due to the removal of the gun ring and bombing gear. As a result, sweepback on the top wing of the Hart Trainer was reduced from 5° to 2.5°. An increase in fin area was also considered but found to be unnecessary in practice. Two further 'interim' machines were built (K3474, K2475) before the first 13 production examples were ordered through Contract No. 246227/33 (K3146-K3158).

Further production orders that were forthcoming proved to be a strain on Hawker's production facilities. Licence production was therefore arranged so that Vickers could build 65 Hart bombers to Contract No. 198868/32 (K2966-K3030), soon followed by a further 24 through Contract No. 198870/32 (K3031-K3054) awarded to Armstrong Whitworth. Further Hart Trainers built by Hawkers consisted of 21 examples (K3743-K3763), 1 Hart Trainer Special (K4617) and 20 Series 2 (K4751-k4770) for use in Temperate climes. Vickers built 47 Hart Single-Seat Day Bombers (SEDB) under Contract No. 262680/33 (K3808-K3845) and 114 Hart Trainers Special 2A fitted with Tropical radiators (K5784-K5879). Armstrong Whitworth built 50 Hart SEDB and C most of which were completed as Audaxes, Harts Trainer (Interim) and Harts Trainer Special together with two batches of Harts Trainer Special 2A, 167 (K4886-K5052) and 136 (K6415-K6550) respectively.

Meanwhile, the Hart featured prominently in the RAF of the mid-thirties, and also went to equip Nos. 6, 12, 15, 39, 40, 60, 142 Squadrons while units of the Royal Auxiliary Air Force (RAuxAF) flying the Hart included Nos. 500, 501, 503, 600, 601, 602, 603, 605, 609, 610, 611. Use of the Hart Fighter by a Flight of No. 23 has already been mentioned above.

Harts Overseas
It might seem surprising that while the single-seat Fury, which clearly displayed its ancestry in the Hart, and other derivatives within the same family of aircraft found such a wide export market, the Hart itself did not fare well in this regard. One reason that has often been offered for this was that Hawker did not have the facilities or finance available to support its export sales.

The first overseas customer for the Hart was Estonia, with an order for eight examples (146-153) which were delivered in the autumn of 1932. These were equipped with interchangeable wheel and float undercarriage, the latter arrangement having been successfully tested on another Hart offspring, the naval version known as the Osprey. Little is known about the fate of these aircraft.

Far better known is the history of the Swedish Harts. Sweden was one of the countries visited between 1931 and 1932 by a Hawker's demonstration team, and following further inspections by Swedish officials at Filton and Brooklands where various Hart test-beds were undergoing trials, an order was placed for

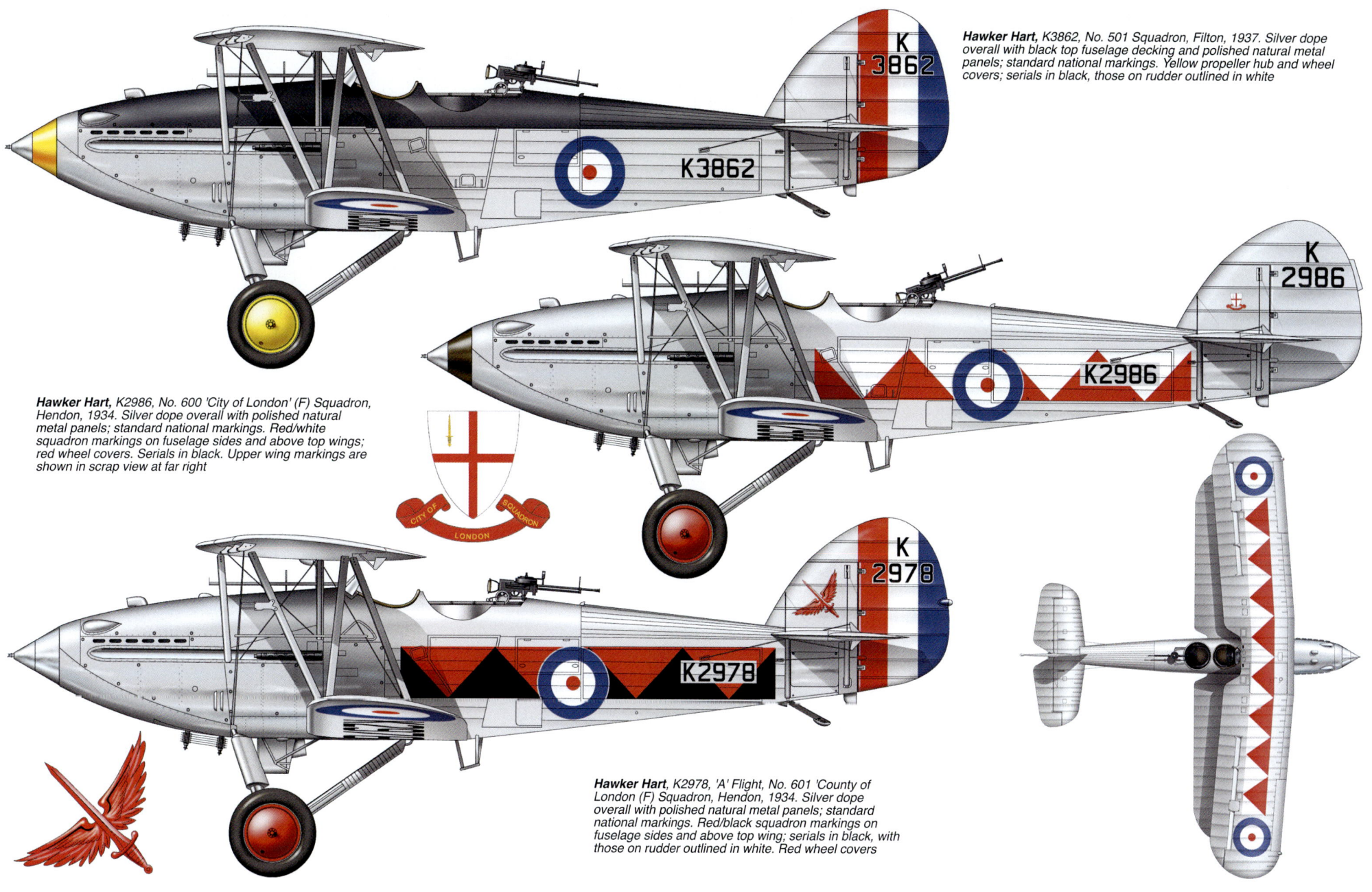

Hawker Hart, K3862, No. 501 Squadron, Filton, 1937. Silver dope overall with black top fuselage decking and polished natural metal panels; standard national markings. Yellow propeller hub and wheel covers; serials in black, those on rudder outlined in white

Hawker Hart, K2986, No. 600 'City of London' (F) Squadron, Hendon, 1934. Silver dope overall with polished natural metal panels; standard national markings. Red/white squadron markings on fuselage sides and above top wings; red wheel covers. Serials in black. Upper wing markings are shown in scrap view at far right

Hawker Hart, K2978, 'A' Flight, No. 601 'County of London (F) Squadron, Hendon, 1934. Silver dope overall with polished natural metal panels; standard national markings. Red/black squadron markings on fuselage sides and above top wing; serials in black, with those on rudder outlined in white. Red wheel covers

three pattern aircraft (1301-1303) for the Swedish Air Force (SAS). These were to be delivered during 1934, powered by a 580hp Bristol Pegasus IM2 radial engine. A licence was also acquired for the construction of a further 42 examples by ASJA, Götaverken and CFM in Sweden, these to be powered by a licence-built 550hp Nohab Pegasus IU2 engine. Swedish Harts were identified by the designation B 4 for the former and B 4A for the latter, while two examples fitted with a Bristol Perseus XI engine of 755hp were designated B 4B.

Serials in SAS ran from 701 to 745 and were built as follows: Hawker – 701 to 703, CFM – 704 to 712, 728 to 739; ASJA – 713 to 724, 740 to 745; Götaverken – 725 to 727. They were operated between 1936 and 1947 by F1 at Västerâs, F4 at Fröson, F6 at Karlsborg, F7 at Såtenäs, F8 at Barkarby, F9 at Säve, F10 at Ängelholm, F11 at Nyköping, F12 at Kalmar, F17 at Ronneby and F21 at Luleå. It must be stressed, however, that only the first four units (and particularly the first three) were ever equipped with the Hart in great numbers, the other units fielding between one and three examples in combination with other types.

The Swedish Hart differed from the original not only in its power plant but also in various other details including its armament, consisting of a Browning 8mm M/22 gun fixed on the starboard side (instead of port) and a similar hand-operated gun in the rear cockpit, together with a larger area fin and rudder.

When Russia attacked Finland in November 1939, F19 was set up on 19 December 1939 by Swedish volunteer pilots under the command of Major Hugo Beckhammar equipped with aircraft purchased with money collected among the Swedish public. Four Hart B 4 bombers (a fifth being added later) formed part of the unit which was also equipped with Gloster Gladiators (see SAMI Vol.7/1, January 2001). The Harts had their baptism of fire on 12 January 1940 when they flew a reconnaissance and ground-attack mission against troops and the airbase at Märkajärvi, Salmijärvi, Salla.

During this attack the Gladiators shot down one I-15 and destroyed a second on the ground, while two further I-15s were credited to Harts flown by Överstelöjtnant Per E. Sterner and Löjtnant Nils Åke Mörne, also destroyed on the ground. Three of the Harts, however, were lost during that attack, two of which in an air-to-air collision. Sterner became a Soviet prisoner of war, while his observer Löjtnant Anders Zachau, was killed. Fänrik Arne Jung also became a Soviet POW but his observer Furir Matti Sundsten managed to ski back to the Finnish lines. The third, flown by Fänrik Gunnar Färnström, was attacked by three I-15s and suffered enough damage to force the pilot make an emergency landing. Another attack was mounted on the night of 18-19 February with another I-15 credited as destroyed on the ground awarded to Löjtnant Nils Åke Mörne.

A final sortie by Mörne and Färnström took place on 12 March when the two Harts attacked road traffic. The following day the Winter War ended and on 29 March one of the bombers flew back to Sweden, followed by the second survivor the day after. The five Harts operated with Finnish markings, and carried the codes R, Z, Y, X and M on their rudders.

Four ex-RAF Harts are reportedly to have been loaned to the Yugoslav Air Force in 1931 while a number of other ex-RAF machines were supplied to South Africa and Rhodesia just prior to the Second World War.

Epilogue
The RAF Museum's Hart has possibly survived through its long association with Hawker. The parent company and Rolls-Royce decided to buy back ex-RAF aircraft for engine test flying. The first was G-ABMR, which flew with every version of Kestrel engine ever produced between 1930 and 1939. During the war it was assigned a number of photographic sorties and was also used as transport for ferry pilots. During the post-war period it flew in a magnificent all-blue finish and was later painted in No. 57 Squadron colours carrying the serial J9941.

Hawker's own G-ABMR after being repainted to represent J9941 of No. 57 Squadron. It is now preserved in the RAF Museum, Hendon (Hawker Siddeley Aviation)

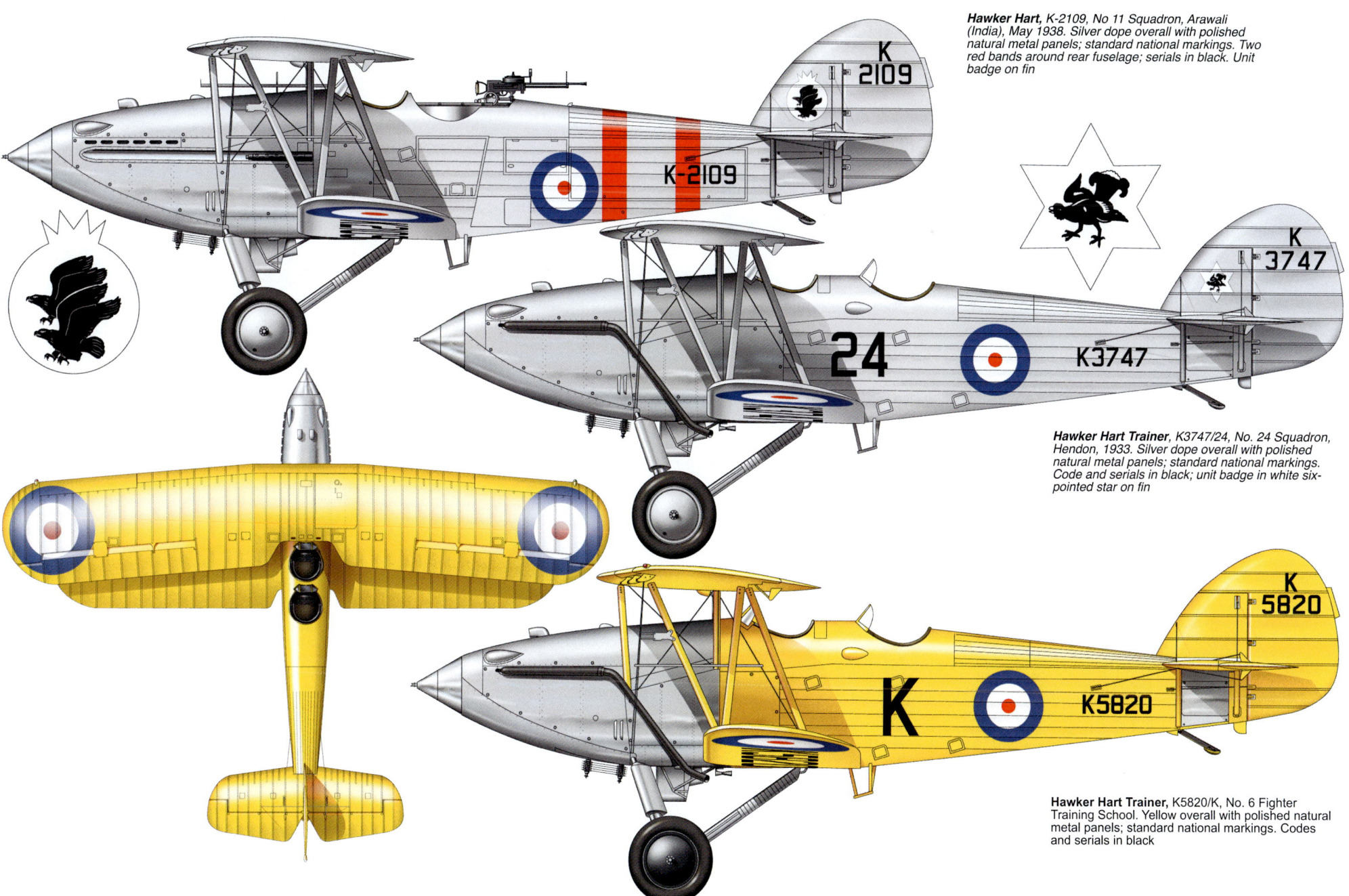

Hawker Hart, K-2109, No 11 Squadron, Arawali (India), May 1938. Silver dope overall with polished natural metal panels; standard national markings. Two red bands around rear fuselage; serials in black. Unit badge on fin

Hawker Hart Trainer, K3747/24, No. 24 Squadron, Hendon, 1933. Silver dope overall with polished natural metal panels; standard national markings. Code and serials in black; unit badge in white six-pointed star on fin

Hawker Hart Trainer, K5820/K, No. 6 Fighter Training School. Yellow overall with polished natural metal panels; standard national markings. Codes and serials in black

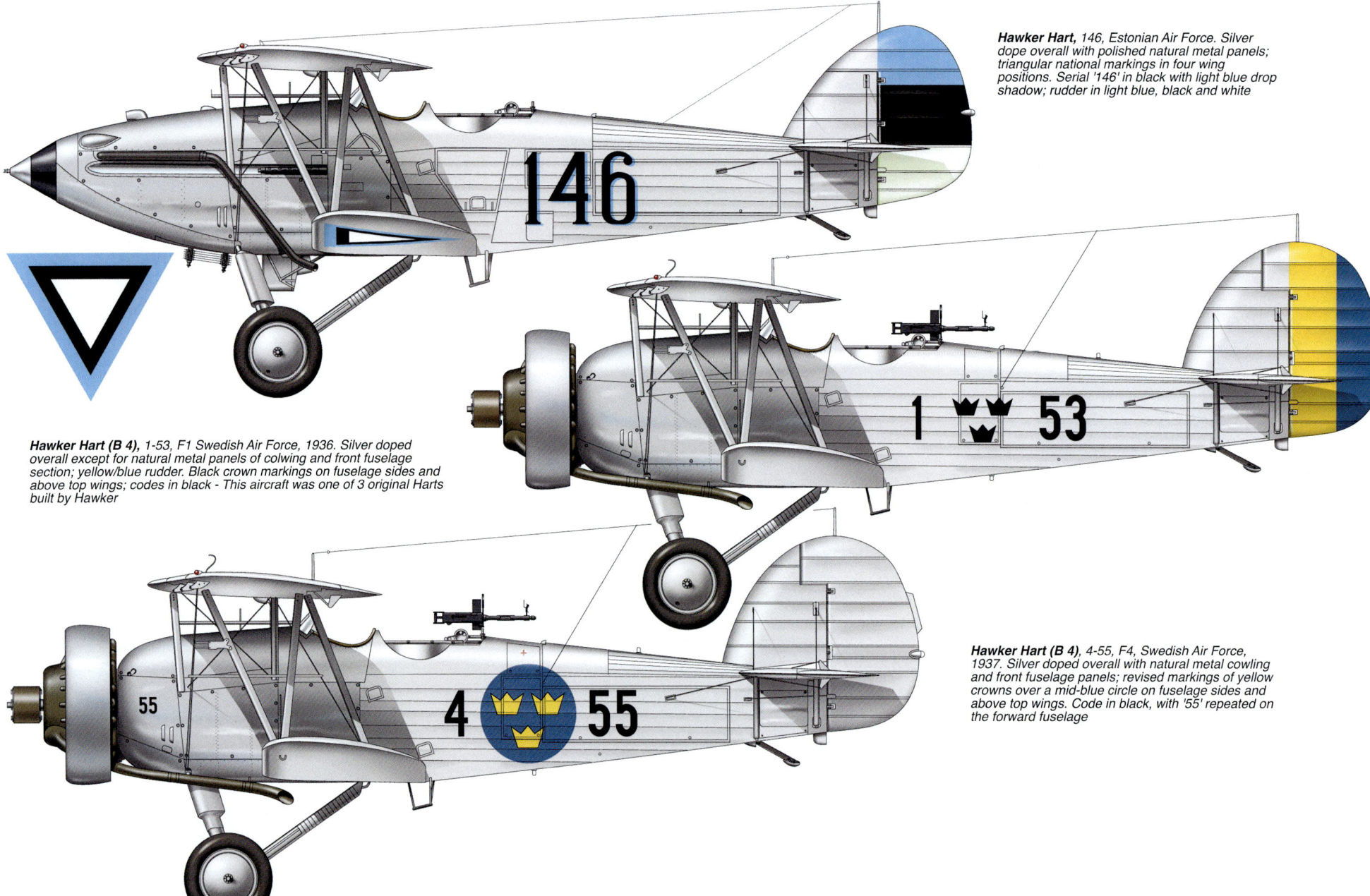

Hawker Hart, *146, Estonian Air Force. Silver dope overall with polished natural metal panels; triangular national markings in four wing positions. Serial '146' in black with light blue drop shadow; rudder in light blue, black and white*

Hawker Hart (B 4), *1-53, F1 Swedish Air Force, 1936. Silver doped overall except for natural metal panels of cowling and front fuselage section; yellow/blue rudder. Black crown markings on fuselage sides and above top wings; codes in black - This aircraft was one of 3 original Harts built by Hawker*

Hawker Hart (B 4), *4-55, F4, Swedish Air Force, 1937. Silver doped overall with natural metal cowling and front fuselage panels; revised markings of yellow crowns over a mid-blue circle on fuselage sides and above top wings. Code in black, with '55' repeated on the forward fuselage*

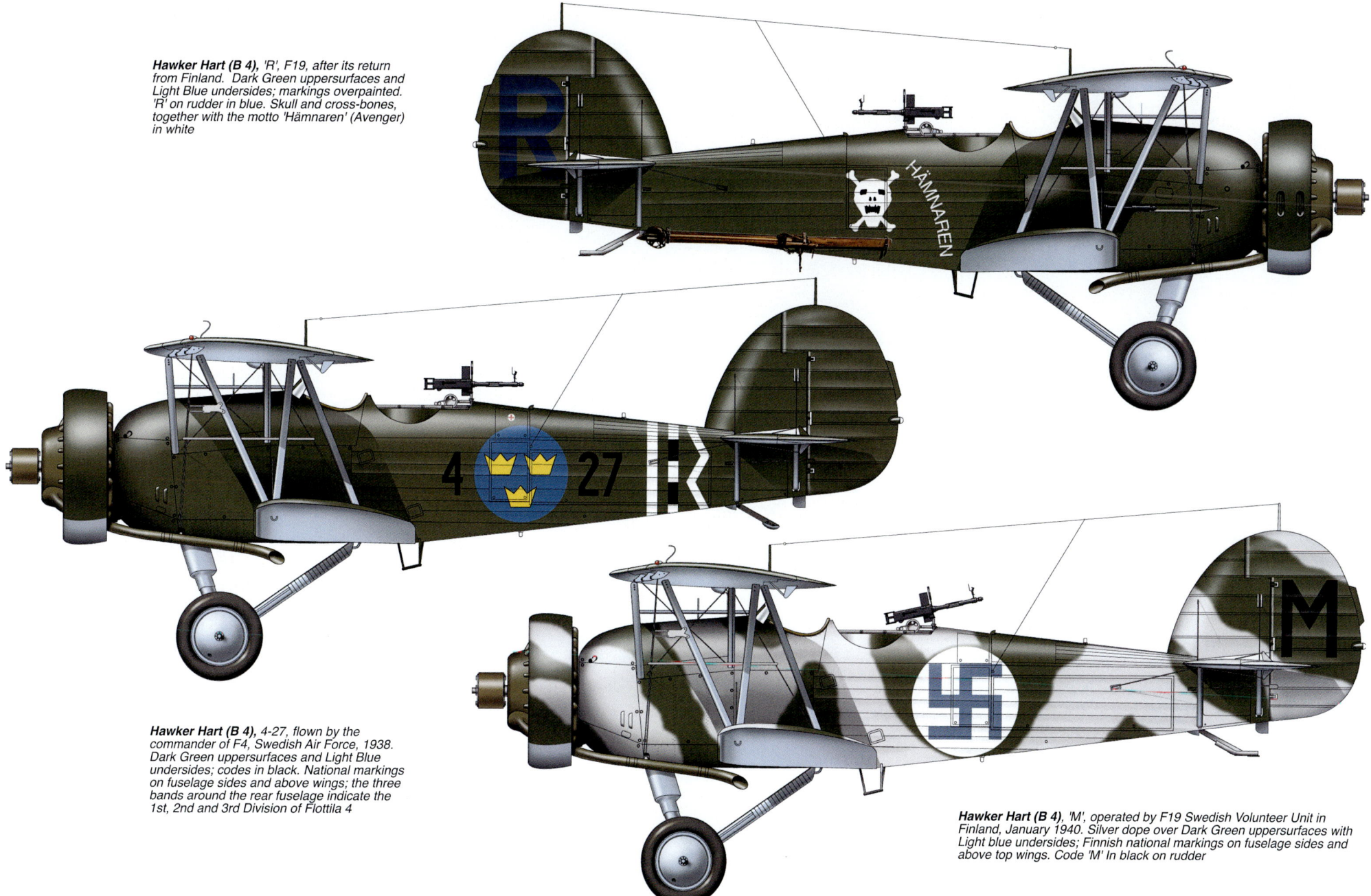

Hawker Hart (B 4), 'R', F19, after its return from Finland. Dark Green uppersurfaces and Light Blue undersides; markings overpainted. 'R' on rudder in blue. Skull and cross-bones, together with the motto 'Hämnaren' (Avenger) in white

Hawker Hart (B 4), 4-27, flown by the commander of F4, Swedish Air Force, 1938. Dark Green uppersurfaces and Light Blue undersides; codes in black. National markings on fuselage sides and above wings; the three bands around the rear fuselage indicate the 1st, 2nd and 3rd Division of Flottila 4

Hawker Hart (B 4), 'M', operated by F19 Swedish Volunteer Unit in Finland, January 1940. Silver dope over Dark Green uppersurfaces with Light blue undersides; Finnish national markings on fuselage sides and above top wings. Code 'M' In black on rudder

ANTI-CAMOUFLAGE SWISS BF 109 D-1/E-3

Messerschmitt Bf109D-1, Wk.Nr.2300, J-305, January 1939. Wavy top camouflage delivery scheme in RLM 70/71 with RLM 65 undersides. Code J-305 in white on fuselage sides. Red disks with white crosses in four wing positions. White cross on top half of rudder in red

Messerschmitt Bf109D-1, Wk.Nr. 2303, J-308, in markings introduced in May 1939. RLM 71 overall with RLM 65 undersides. Code J-308 in white. Red panels 130cm wide on fuselage sides and around wings (top and bottom) with white crosses superimposed. White cross on top of red rudder

Messerschmitt Bf109D-1, Wk.Nr. 2302 J-307 in the full neutality markings introduced on 16 September 1944. RLM 71 upper surfaces with RLM 65 undersides and white nose section. White codes on fuselage sides. Red panel on fuselage sides and wings carrying a white cross. Red rudder with white cross superimposed

Messerschmitt Bf109E-3, Wk.Nr. 2191, J-333, 1939. Original delivery scheme of RLM70/71 upper surfaces in a wavy pattern, with RLM 65 undersides. Codes are white; national markings in the form of a round red disk with a white cross in four wing positions. White cross on red panel on rudder. Note original MG25 machine guns retained

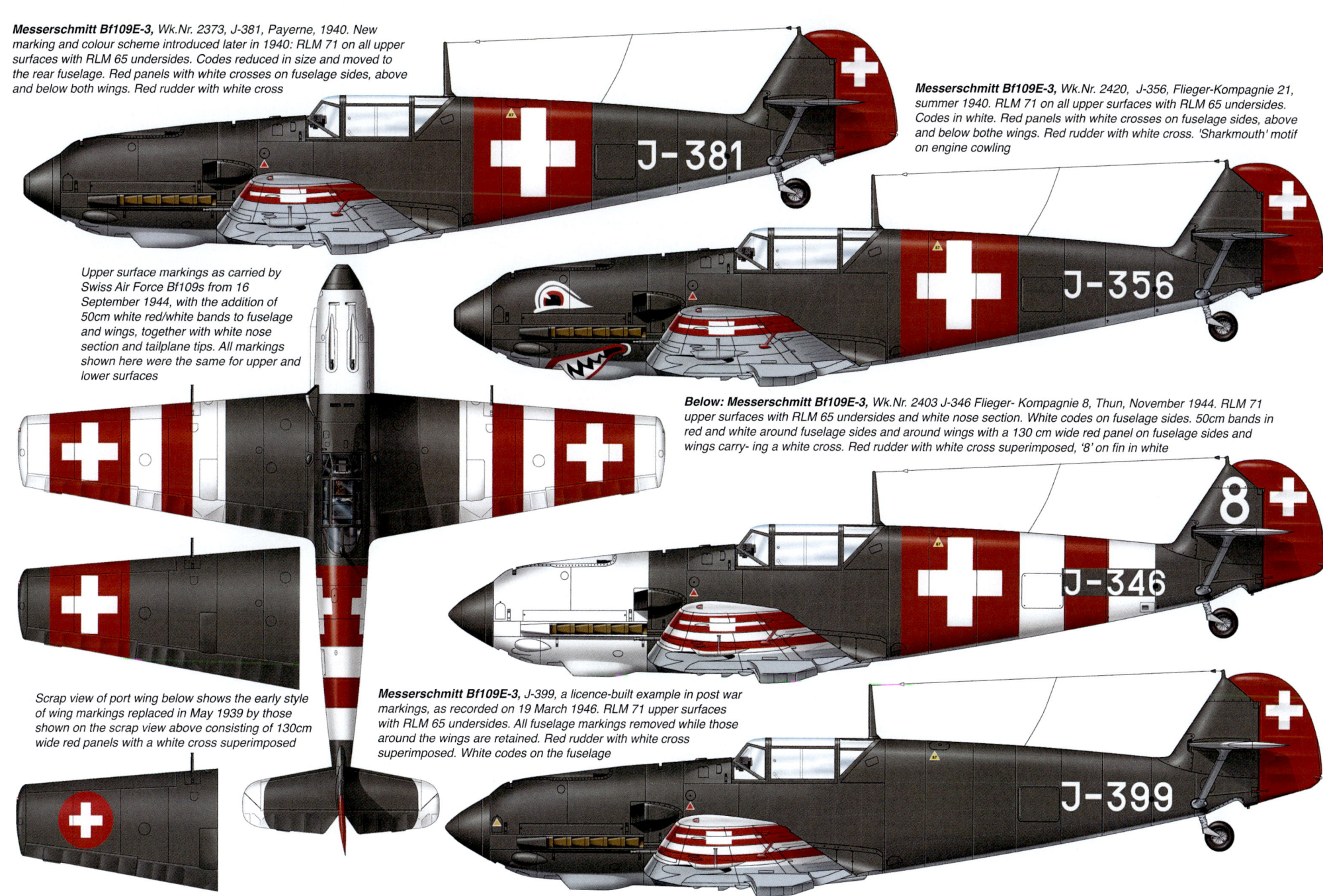

A Japanese Swallow – The Kawasaki Ki-61 Hien

When the Ki-61 Hien started to appear in some numbers, the Allies believed that it was a Japanese copy of the German Messerschmitt Bf 109. The only similarity, however, was in the origins of the engine that powered the two aircraft. Code-named 'Tony' by the Americans, the Ki-61 proved to be a radical change in design philosophy in more ways than one — though not in the eyes of the Allies, maybe! To Japanese aviation it was as much of a milestone as was the A6M Zero during the earlier part of the conflict. Had it not suffered so badly from poor standards of its license-produced engine, the Hien would have probably left a much more impressive mark to its name.

Fighter tactics of the Imperial Japanese Army Air Force were based on the concept of superb manoeuvrability and pilot skill — these, it was believed, were sufficient to give a well-trained fighter pilot the edge on any opponent. However, it was becoming increasingly obvious from the lessons learnt during the early stages of the war in Europe (and the Battle of Britain, in particular) that speed and climb were becoming determining factors in aerial dog-fighting.

These qualities, combined with a highly manoeuvrable aircraft, were changing the tactics of aerial warfare of the major combatants. Whoever had the advantage of altitude and speed enjoyed a distinct advantage. During the mid-thirties, the Kawasaki design team had already began to grow closer to such new ways of thinking and was looking towards liquid-cooled in-line engine as the definite power plant for propeller-driven aircraft of the future. By 1937 they had acquired a license for the production of one of the world's most advanced engine of its time, the Daimler-Benz DB601A, but official interest was still lacking.

By 1940, even diehards in high official circles had to accept the changing concepts of fighter tactics. Although the Japanese aircraft industry was, by that time, heavily committed in the production of the A6M "Zero" as its main fighter aircraft, the need for a more modern and efficient fighter became a matter of urgency.,Thus Kawasaki received instructions in February 1940 to begin design work around the DB601A in-line engine of two fighter aircraft, one of which was to be a special cannon-armed version. The projects were assigned the designations Ki-60 and Ki-61. The former, which was to have the heavier armament, was assigned a higher priority. Time lost in obtaining the license production of the DB601A off the ground had to be recuperated and a Kawasaki team visited the Daimler-Benz works in Germany in April to study production techniques and the adaptability of this engine to Japanese production facilities.

Detail design and production of three Ki-60 prototypes moved at a fantastically fast pace. An imported DB601A was fitted to the first prototype that turned out to be a superbly compact fighter, heavily armed with two wing-mounted Mauser MG151 20mm cannon and two fuselage 12.7mm machine guns firing through the propeller arc. By March 1941 the Ki-60 was complete but initial flight trials soon showed serious handling problems and the second and third prototypes had their wings enlarged in area.

Meanwhile the design of the Ki-61 was also proceeding and by summer of 1941 the project received top priority keeping Takeo Doi and Shin Owada fully occupied with their new fighter. While the first prototype was under construction, Akashi were working on the Ha-40 engine, the DB601A license version, with initial bench testing taking place in July 1941. By the end of that year Akashi delivered two pre-production engines and a further eight examples for the Ki-61 programme. By the second week of December 1941 the first Ki-61 was complete, including all engine fits and from the results of the first flights it became immediately obvious that this aircraft was going to be a superb all-rounder.

Speeds of up to 367mph were reached at the manufacturer's test facility at Kagamigahara early in 1942. Notwithstanding the use of the same engine as in the Ki-60, both speeds and manoeuvrability were markedly improved in the much larger Ki-61. Long term material procurement and mass-production jigs were already at an advanced stage.

The Ki-61-II flown by Maj Kobayashi, Commanding Officer of the 244th Sentai marked with 14 kills below the cockpit and the blue stripe along the fuselage. Full colour details can be found in the accompanying colour art profile

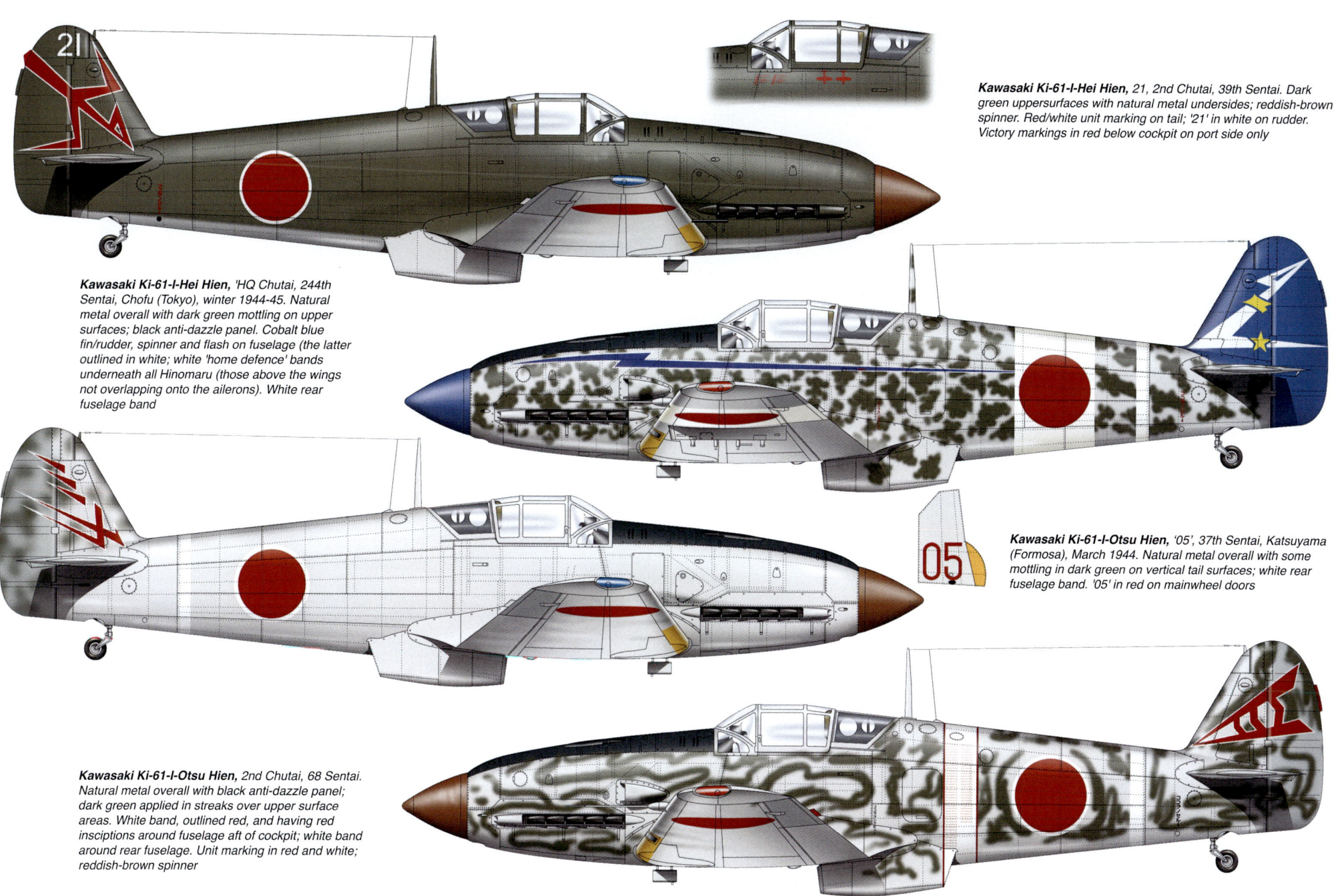

Kawasaki Ki-61-I-Hei Hien, 21, 2nd Chutai, 39th Sentai. Dark green uppersurfaces with natural metal undersides; reddish-brown spinner. Red/white unit marking on tail; '21' in white on rudder. Victory markings in red below cockpit on port side only

Kawasaki Ki-61-I-Hei Hien, 'HQ Chutai, 244th Sentai, Chofu (Tokyo), winter 1944-45. Natural metal overall with dark green mottling on upper surfaces; black anti-dazzle panel. Cobalt blue fin/rudder, spinner and flash on fuselage (the latter outlined in white; white 'home defence' bands underneath all Hinomaru (those above the wings not overlapping onto the ailerons). White rear fuselage band

Kawasaki Ki-61-I-Otsu Hien, '05', 37th Sentai, Katsuyama (Formosa), March 1944. Natural metal overall with some mottling in dark green on vertical tail surfaces; white rear fuselage band. '05' in red on mainwheel doors

Kawasaki Ki-61-I-Otsu Hien, 2nd Chutai, 68 Sentai. Natural metal overall with black anti-dazzle panel; dark green applied in streaks over upper surface areas. White band, outlined red, and having red inscriptions around fuselage aft of cockpit; white band around rear fuselage. Unit marking in red and white; reddish-brown spinner

One of the many Ki-61s captured by American forces, in this case a Ki-61-I found in a damaged state at Okinawa

The initial elation soon cooled down due to a series of nasty accidents involving some of the other eleven prototypes, including some incidents which remained unexplained even after lengthy inquiries. This did not affect the full impetus of the programme and advanced production got under way just the same. Prototypes and early production aircraft nearly all differed in detail, due to the extensive experimentations, sometimes on even the most minute details. For example, the thirteenth Ki-61 — the first example to be built on production jigs — was fitted with a side-opening canopy similar to that used by the Bf 109. This canopy came off its hinges in flight, squashing the pilot into the cockpit; miraculously, major Aramaki made a perfect landing on instruments only, not being in a position to see where he was going! In spite of these shortcomings, the Army had no hesitation in accepting the type into its inventory as the Army Type 3 Fighter Model 1.

The Ki-61 Described

Of cantilever, low-wing monoplane design, the Ki-61 was of all-metal flush-riveted construction with fully retractable mainwheels and (on early models) tailwheel. The wing was built on three spars with the pilot's seat being positioned on the rear one. Each wing housed a 200-litre self-sealing fuel tank and included internal plumbing for supplementary external underwing tanks for a further 200 litres.

The forward section of the fuselage consisted of the engine and its ancillary equipment, fuselage mounted guns and ammunition tanks followed by the fire bulkhead for the cockpit to which the pilot's instruments were attached. On top of the control panel was fitted a standard gun sight with flat optical sight. The forward windscreen panel consisted of armoured glass, while pilot protection in the form of 13mm armour plating was fitted to the headrest and seat's back — quite a luxury on Japanese aircraft of the time!

Access to the aircraft was by climbing up a footrest that retracted into the wing trailing edge fillet on the port side, and a spring-loaded handhold halfway up the fuselage; the canopy slid aft. Just behind the pilot was positioned the fuselage fuel tank of 165 litres' capacity and a Type 99-III radio pack. A port fuselage access panel was positioned between these two.

Standard production aircraft were powered by a Kawasaki Ha-40, 12-cylinder, inverted-vee engine which produced 1,175hp. Armament consisted of two 12.7mm Ho-103 machine guns in the forward fuselage and two 7.7mm Type 89 machine guns in the wings. Wing loading was still relatively high at 147.5kg/m2 especially when compared to its other competitor of the time, the Ki-43 Hayabusa, with which some odious comparisons were made during its debut. However the two aircraft should not have been compared as they were built with completely different concepts in mind.

Into Action

The first taste of action for the Ki-61 Hien came on April 18, 1942. The type was not yet in squadron service but one of the prototypes was called during a test flight to intercept a formation of B-25 Mitchells. These were J.H. Doolittle's bomber force that had taken off from USS Hornet to bomb mainland Japan. The Ki-61 gave chase but only managed a burst of gunfire at very long range with no apparent results.

As the Hien began to leave the production lines in some numbers the wing armament fit varied between the prototype's 7.7mm and the larger 12.7mm. Fitted with the latter armament, the aircraft was known as the Ki-61-otsu while with the former guns it received the official denomination of Ki-61-I-ko.

The 68th Sentai was the first to receive the new Ki-61s soon followed by the 78th. The working-up period was characterised by various teething problems especially related to the engine. The 68th was assigned to Wewak, New Guinea, while the 78th went to Rabaul in New Britain. With the increased tempo of production during 1943 more Sentais were formed and slowly the new mount began to be appreciated by its crews. There was no doubt that it was a strong, well-armed and fast fighter but not one to be thrown about the sky with ease. In the Philippines the 17th, 18th and 19th Sentai were formed in February 1944. For defence of the home islands (August 1944) the 56th and 105th were formed while the 59th later changed its Ki-43s for the Ki-61. Home defence was the responsibility of the 224th Sentai together with the 28th.

The demand for heavier firepower became more urgent when the Ki-61 began to encounter the newer generations of US fighters. The 20mm Ho-5 cannon was

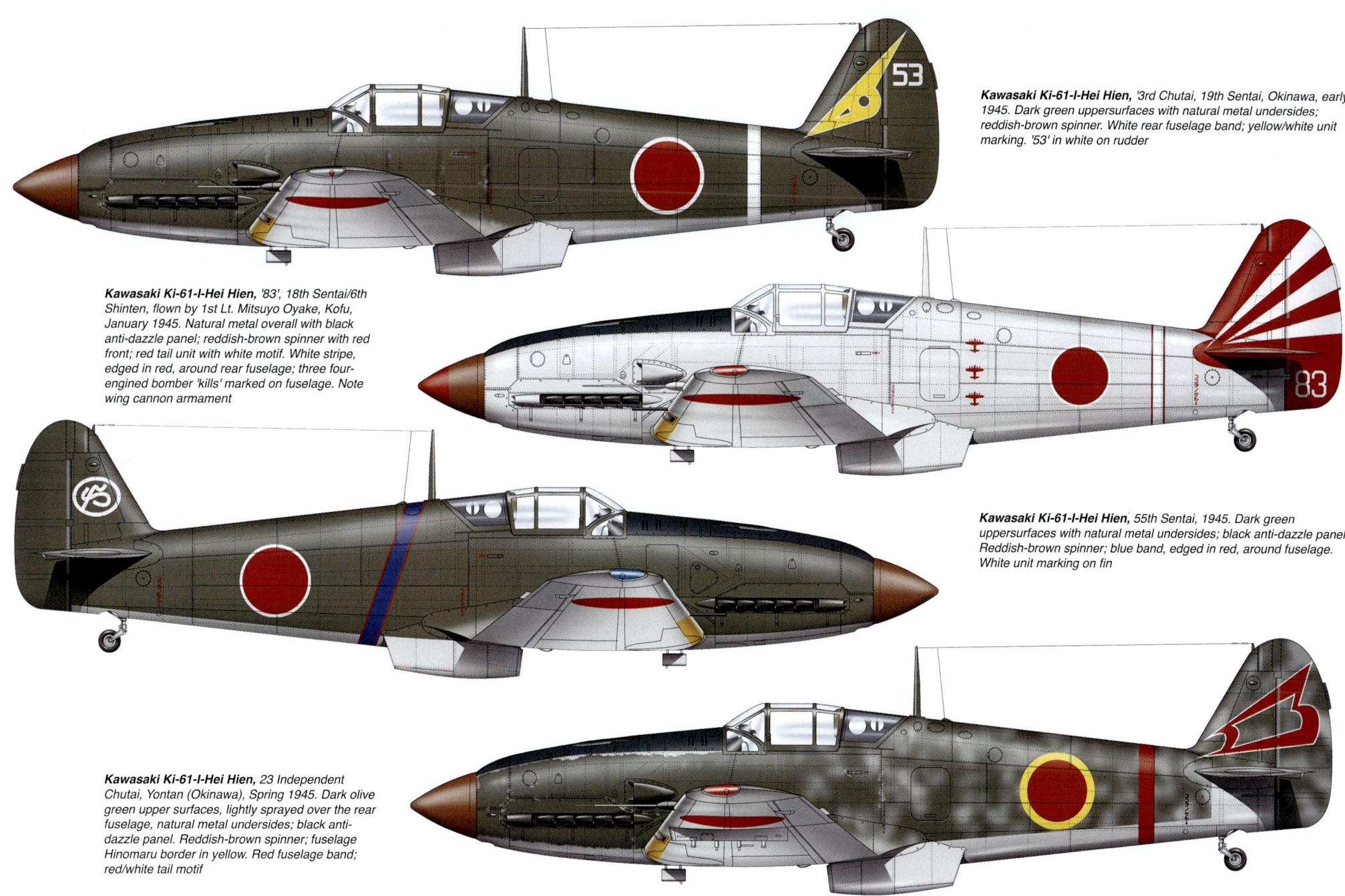

Kawasaki Ki-61-I-Hei Hien, '3rd Chutai, 19th Sentai, Okinawa, early 1945. Dark green uppersurfaces with natural metal undersides; reddish-brown spinner. White rear fuselage band; yellow/white unit marking. '53' in white on rudder

Kawasaki Ki-61-I-Hei Hien, '83', 18th Sentai/6th Shinten, flown by 1st Lt. Mitsuyo Oyake, Kofu, January 1945. Natural metal overall with black anti-dazzle panel; reddish-brown spinner with red front; red tail unit with white motif. White stripe, edged in red, around rear fuselage; three four-engined bomber 'kills' marked on fuselage. Note wing cannon armament

Kawasaki Ki-61-I-Hei Hien, 55th Sentai, 1945. Dark green uppersurfaces with natural metal undersides; black anti-dazzle panel. Reddish-brown spinner; blue band, edged in red, around fuselage. White unit marking on fin

Kawasaki Ki-61-I-Hei Hien, 23 Independent Chutai, Yontan (Okinawa), Spring 1945. Dark olive green upper surfaces, lightly sprayed over the rear fuselage, natural metal undersides; black anti-dazzle panel. Reddish-brown spinner; fuselage Hinomaru border in yellow. Red fuselage band; red/white tail motif

More war booty, Ki-61 'Tonys' of the 19th Sentai at Luzon, among other Japanese types; 1945

nearly ready for mass production and eventual replacement for the fuselage guns of the Hien but in the meantime the early versions of the Ki-61 began to be converted, even on the field, to take Mauser MG151 20mm cannon in the wings. Japan received from Germany (via submarine) 800 such weapons in August 1943 that went to arm over 380 Hiens. Early in the following year the Ki-61-I-KAI-hei(c) armed with fuselage-mounted 20mm cannon was available and by mid-summer of 1944 the earlier versions had all been withdrawn from front line use. The type was identifiable from the slightly lengthened engine cowling.

The additional weight sacrificed little of the Ki-61's performance, which in any case was more than compensated for by the higher firepower. However, Japan's reserves of materials and even of skilled labour were becoming scarcer and the standard of aircraft production fell to miserable levels with tragic consequences.

The next version to appear was the Ki-61-I-KAI-tei(d) which reverted to the 12.7mm fuselage guns but housed two 30mm Ho-105 cannon in the wings. This fit turned out to be very disappointing in performance and was soon phased out of production. This fall in quality was further complicated by a fall in production rate from a peak of over 200 examples a month to a mere 50 by the end of 1944.

A Better Hien

No sooner had the H-40 engine entered production that attention was turned to a higher-rated version, the Ha-140 of 1,500hp. The installation of the new engine meant that the Hien fuselage had to be slightly redesigned around the nose area. The opportunity was taken to revise the shape of the windscreen. The wings, too, were slightly increased in area to benefit from the increased power at higher altitudes, but basically retained the plan form of the original Ki-61.

The first prototype was ready in August 1943 but engine development had not moved at the same pace as that of the airframe. In December the Ha-140 was installed and the Ki-61-II, as this version was now designated, began flight trials. It was a surprise to everybody concerned in the project — in a negative sense! It turned out to be a total disappointment in both handling and performance. It was obvious that not enough time had been allocated to proper design of the wings. Unable to afford more time for further wing redesign, standard Ki-61 wings were fitted to the ninth prototype, which also had an enlarged fin. The Ki-61-II-KAI was a resounding success — speed went up to 380mph at 20,000ft. Again the initial production examples had both 12.77m and 20mm wing armament and were sub-designated -ko and -otsu respectively. Without doubt, this was a superb fighting machine.

However engine and airframe production did not go apace and twice as many airframes than the number of available engines had been built by the end of 1944. The Ha-140 continued to prove temperamental in service use and the future of this very promising aircraft was cut short when the decision was taken to fit the remaining aircraft with radial engines, producing the Ki-100 (Type 5) fighter.

Some Ki-61-IIs did eventually reach operational units. Although pilots had nothing but praise for the aircraft when everything went smoothly, they complained bitterly when the engine began to play up. Another frequent complaint was the inadequate rear view that was eventually solved by modifying one example with an all-round vision canopy. This change arrived too late to be implemented in the Hien but it was put to good use on its successor, the Ki-100.

Had the Japanese aircraft industry got to grips with in-line engine production and development earlier, maybe this story would have ended very differently. Service tradition being given preference to the old but proven product during the late 30s was the main cause of this delay in modernising equipment and production techniques. Still, the Hien left an indelible mark in Japanese aviation history and still proves to be a very popular modelling subject due to its clean and graceful lines, not to mention the fantastic colour schemes and markings which adorned this fighter throughout its service career.

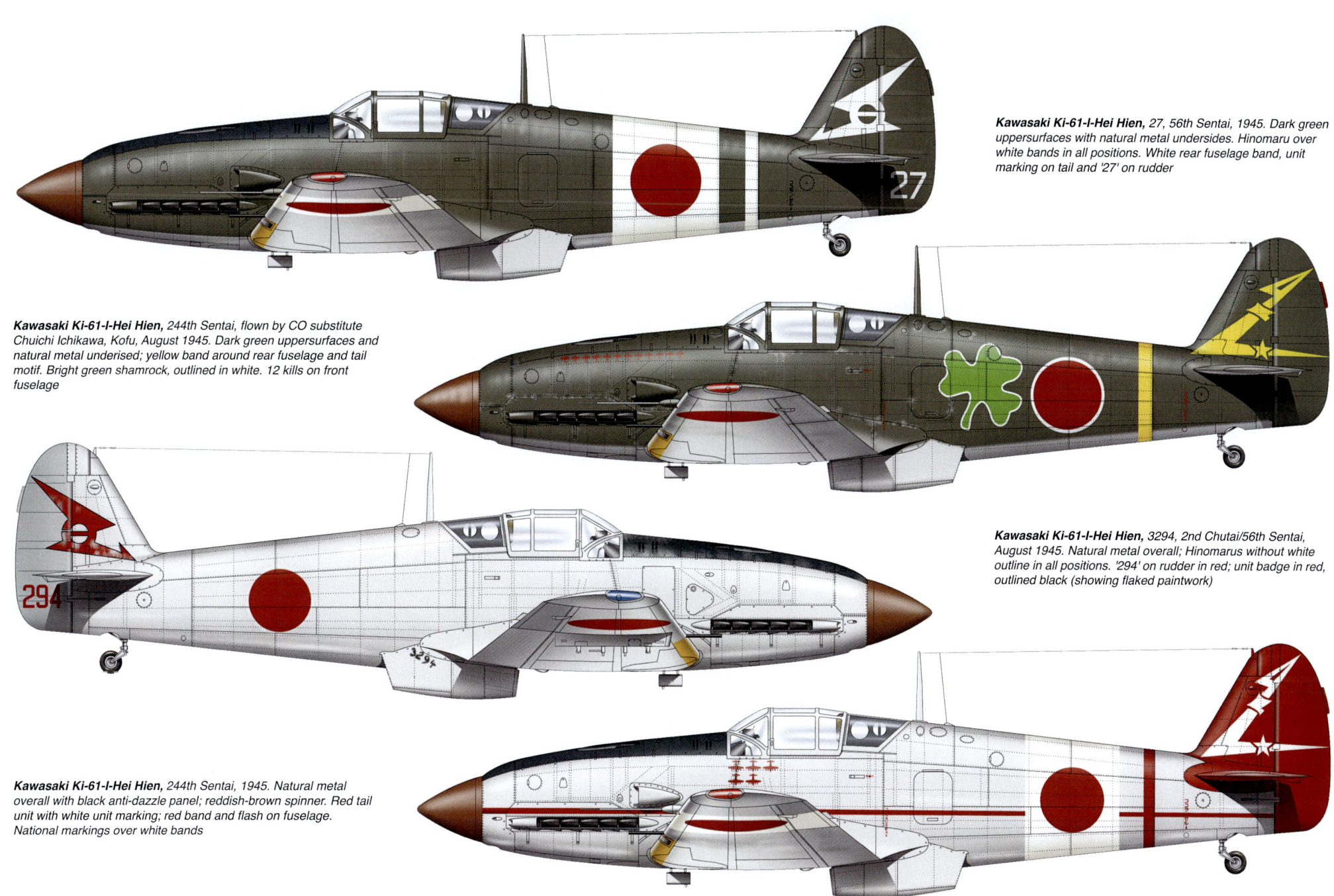

Kawasaki Ki-61-I-Hei Hien, 27, 56th Sentai, 1945. Dark green uppersurfaces with natural metal undersides. Hinomaru over white bands in all positions. White rear fuselage band, unit marking on tail and '27' on rudder

Kawasaki Ki-61-I-Hei Hien, 244th Sentai, flown by CO substitute Chuichi Ichikawa, Kofu, August 1945. Dark green uppersurfaces and natural metal underised; yellow band around rear fuselage and tail motif. Bright green shamrock, outlined in white. 12 kills on front fuselage

Kawasaki Ki-61-I-Hei Hien, 3294, 2nd Chutai/56th Sentai, August 1945. Natural metal overall; Hinomarus without white outline in all positions. '294' on rudder in red; unit badge in red, outlined black (showing flaked paintwork)

Kawasaki Ki-61-I-Hei Hien, 244th Sentai, 1945. Natural metal overall with black anti-dazzle panel; reddish-brown spinner. Red tail unit with white unit marking; red band and flash on fuselage. National markings over white bands

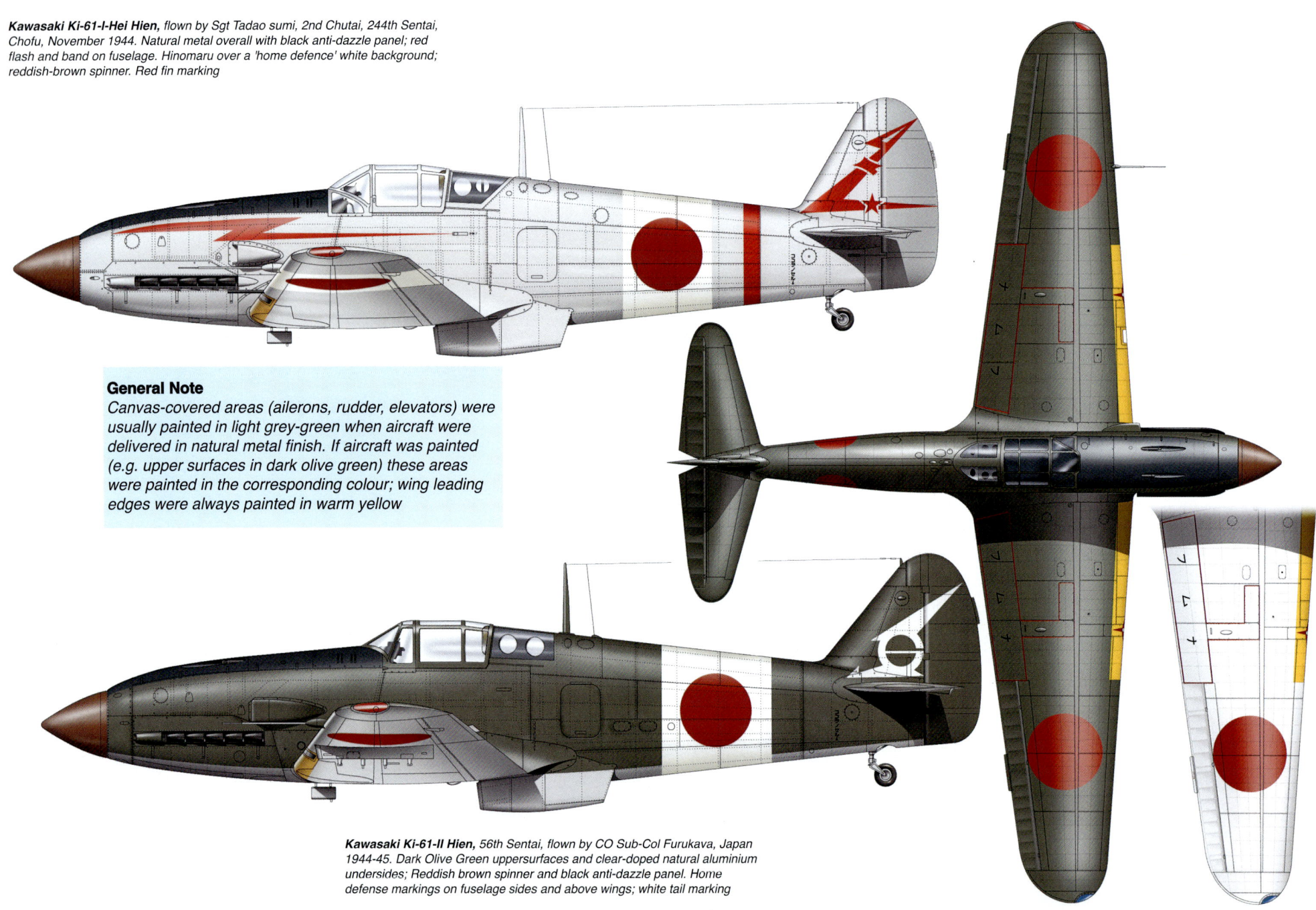

Kawasaki Ki-61-I-Hei Hien, *flown by Sgt Tadao sumi, 2nd Chutai, 244th Sentai, Chofu, November 1944. Natural metal overall with black anti-dazzle panel; red flash and band on fuselage. Hinomaru over a 'home defence' white background; reddish-brown spinner. Red fin marking*

General Note
Canvas-covered areas (ailerons, rudder, elevators) were usually painted in light grey-green when aircraft were delivered in natural metal finish. If aircraft was painted (e.g. upper surfaces in dark olive green) these areas were painted in the corresponding colour; wing leading edges were always painted in warm yellow

Kawasaki Ki-61-II Hien, *56th Sentai, flown by CO Sub-Col Furukava, Japan 1944-45. Dark Olive Green uppersurfaces and clear-doped natural aluminium undersides; Reddish brown spinner and black anti-dazzle panel. Home defense markings on fuselage sides and above wings; white tail marking*

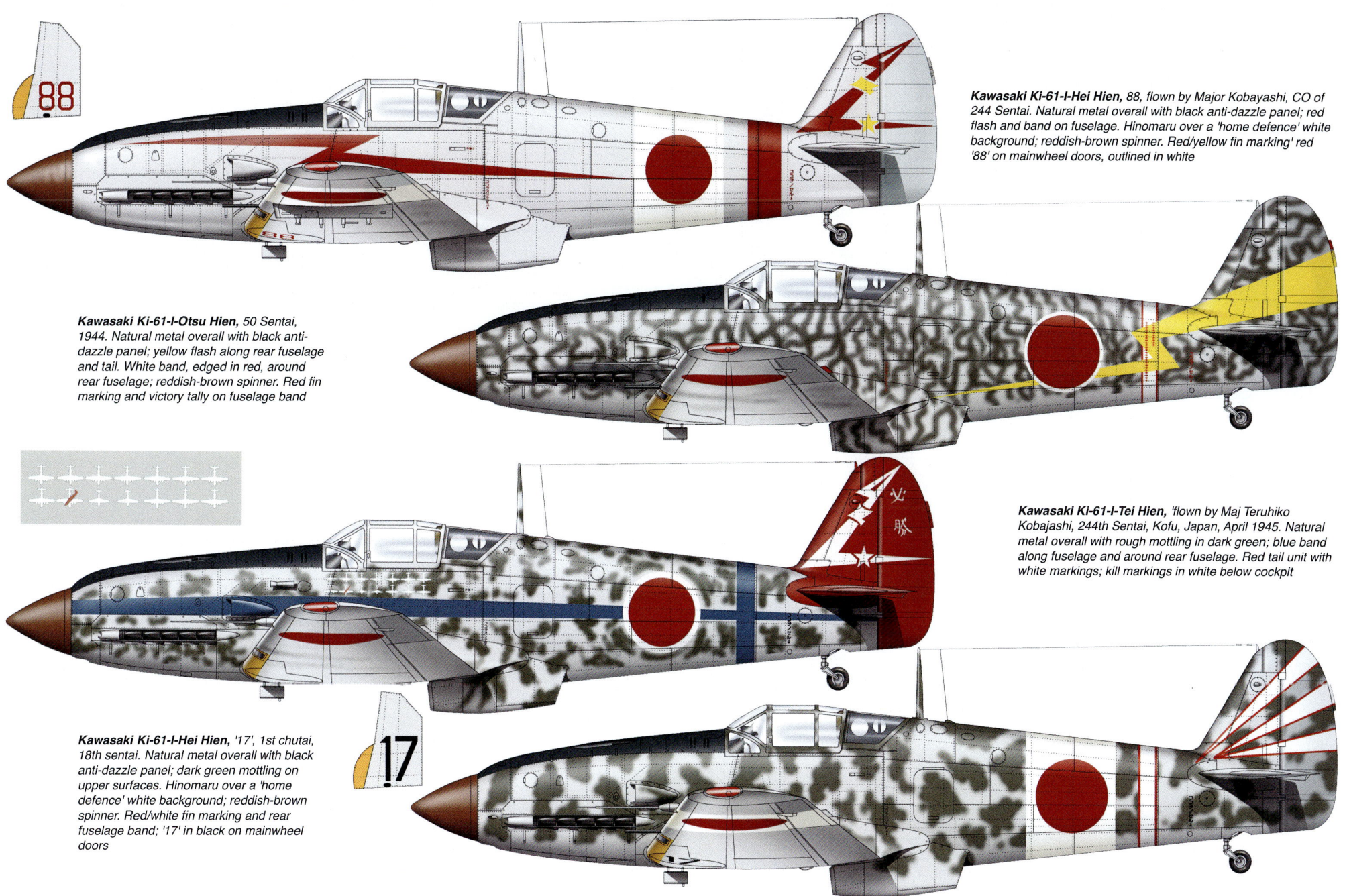

Kawasaki Ki-61-I-Hei Hien, 88, flown by Major Kobayashi, CO of 244 Sentai. Natural metal overall with black anti-dazzle panel; red flash and band on fuselage. Hinomaru over a 'home defence' white background; reddish-brown spinner. Red/yellow fin marking' red '88' on mainwheel doors, outlined in white

Kawasaki Ki-61-I-Otsu Hien, 50 Sentai, 1944. Natural metal overall with black anti-dazzle panel; yellow flash along rear fuselage and tail. White band, edged in red, around rear fuselage; reddish-brown spinner. Red fin marking and victory tally on fuselage band

Kawasaki Ki-61-I-Tei Hien, 'flown by Maj Teruhiko Kobajashi, 244th Sentai, Kofu, Japan, April 1945. Natural metal overall with rough mottling in dark green; blue band along fuselage and around rear fuselage. Red tail unit with white markings; kill markings in white below cockpit

Kawasaki Ki-61-I-Hei Hien, '17', 1st chutai, 18th sentai. Natural metal overall with black anti-dazzle panel; dark green mottling on upper surfaces. Hinomaru over a 'home defence' white background; reddish-brown spinner. Red/white fin marking and rear fuselage band; '17' in black on mainwheel doors

Birth of the Jump Jet – The Harrier

The concept of the Harrier that remains unique in its genre was one of the last private ventures to eventually emerge from Britain's aviation industry, and also the last in which Sir Sidney Camm played a decisive role. Although credit is usually ascribed to the design team he had built up over the previous four decades, Camm decided to initiate such an ambitious project after meeting Dr Stanley Hooker of the Bristol Engine Company early in 1957.

The previous year, Hooker learned of a Frenchman's project for a vertical take-off and landing (VTOL) aeroplane known as the Gyroptère. The design conceived by Michel Wibault featured swivelling compressors on either side of the fuselage fed by air from a conventional gas turbine engine. This led Bristol's design team to embark on a project to study and refine the idea that eventually led to the BE.52, combining the Orpheus and Olympus to provide a ducted fan jet with rotating 'cold' nozzles on either side of the compressor while hot air exited through a conventional central tailpipe.

XP976, one of the four development P.1127 Kestrels (the others being XP972, XP980, XP984). Note the original design of the wings (via Dennis Robinson)

Ralph S. Hooper, senior project engineer at Hawker's, was entrusted with the task of drawing up a layout to embody such an engine, under the designation of P.1127. Very soon, the tail pipe arrangement was changed to one similar to that of the Sea Hawk whereby hot air exited through bifurcated nozzles, except that in this case these were also rotatable. Bristol's engine project became BE.53 so as to incorporate such changes. By August 1957, the Hawker P.1127 became more than a paper project; its design continued to evolve through a programme of very close cooperation between aircraft and engine design engineers.

Unfortunately, this was a time when the infamous Defence White Paper of spring 1957 was wreaking havoc within the British aviation industry, including the scrapping of such advanced fighter projects in favour of unmanned missiles. In such light, Hawker found absolutely no official financial backing and had to look towards NATO as a possible source of funds and, eventually, sales of its VTOL design. If such interest materialised, Hawker could at least aspire for funding through the Mutual Weapons Development Programme (MWDP). Although funding to the tune of 75 percent of development costs for six Bristol BE.53 engines was allocated through MWDP, Hawker had to continue its design project with using company funds after a decision to build two P.1127 prototypes had been – very courageously – taken in April 1959.

The only assistance received at that time by the P.1127 project was the use of Langley's National Aeronautics and Space Administration (NASA) wind tunnel facilities to test its models. However Hawker's determination and foresight began to be rewarded as interest in its project increased from day to day, especially after all design work had been passed on to the Experimental Design Office at Kingston. Draft requirement GOR.345 for a Hunter replacement issued in October 1959 was the first ray of hope that official recognition had finally been achieved, accompanied by a grant of £75,000 supposedly to cover design work that had already been done on the P.1127!

Work at Bristol had moved in great strides, and by March 1960 they had bench-tested an engine earmarked for the P.1127 prototype, which provided 10,000lb installed thrust. At around the same time, Hawker were invited to tender for four development aircraft and in June it also received funding for the two private-venture machines that were nearing completion.

While the two senior test pilots – Bill Bedford and Hugh Merewether – familiarised themselves with the Bell X-14 at Ames Air Force Base (AFB) in the United States, the first engine was delivered to Hawker on 6 May 1960. This was installed in XP831, and on 22 June an official contract for the two prototypes (XP831, XP836) was signed. The first prototype was delivered to Dunsfold on 15 July and ground running of the engine began on 31 August using a specially designed 'silencing pen'. The first Pegasus flight engine arrived on 13 October and installed, and XP831 flew in hover for the first time on 21 October 1960, piloted by Bill Bedford despite having his right leg in a plaster cast, having been declared "fit to fly, tethered mode only" by the RAF's Central Medical Board"! With no markings at all over its bare metal finish, it was tethered at the nose wheel and at each wingtip and apart from its unconventional shape the aircraft also left its mark on those witnessing the flight for its indescribably deafening noise!

Introducing the Kestrel
An order for a further four prototypes (XP972, XP976, XP980, XP984) was issued by the Ministry of Supply on 2 November 1960, meant to serve as evolution aircraft towards the realisation of a military design through the

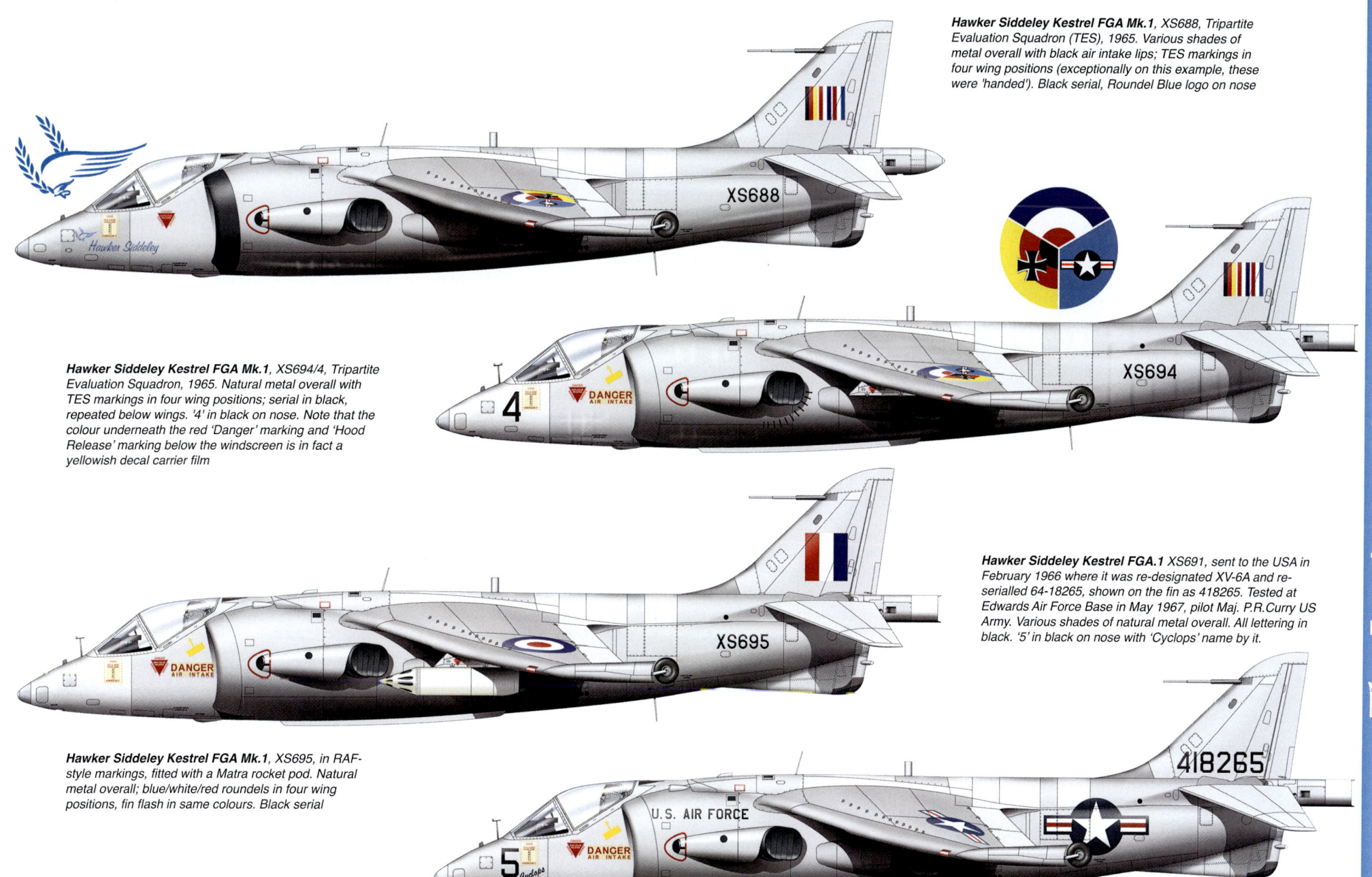

Hawker Siddeley Kestrel FGA Mk.1, XS688, Tripartite Evaluation Squadron (TES), 1965. Various shades of metal overall with black air intake lips; TES markings in four wing positions (exceptionally on this example, these were 'handed'). Black serial, Roundel Blue logo on nose

Hawker Siddeley Kestrel FGA Mk.1, XS694/4, Tripartite Evaluation Squadron, 1965. Natural metal overall with TES markings in four wing positions; serial in black, repeated below wings. '4' in black on nose. Note that the colour underneath the red 'Danger' marking and 'Hood Release' marking below the windscreen is in fact a yellowish decal carrier film

Hawker Siddeley Kestrel FGA Mk.1, XS695, in RAF-style markings, fitted with a Matra rocket pod. Natural metal overall; blue/white/red roundels in four wing positions, fin flash in same colours. Black serial

Hawker Siddeley Kestrel FGA.1 XS691, sent to the USA in February 1966 where it was re-designated XV-6A and re-serialled 64-18265, shown on the fin as 418265. Tested at Edwards Air Force Base in May 1967, pilot Maj. P.R.Curry US Army. Various shades of natural metal overall. All lettering in black. '5' in black on nose with 'Cyclops' name by it.

Harrier GR Mk.1, XV760 of the Harrier Operational Conversion Unit finished in the original high gloss three-tone scheme of Dark Sea Grey/Dark Green/Light Aircraft Grey with high visibility and bright coloured national markings; note the fin code in different styles of numbers. Codes on fin are red, outlined in yellow

increase of engine power, accommodation of operational equipment and the development of wing design. The P.1127's first conventional flight took place on 13 March 1961, piloted by Bill Bedford, lasting 22 minutes. Among the crowd present for the event there was Sir Sydney Camm, George Anderson (Sales Manager), Roy Chaplain (Deputy Chief Designer) and Fred Sutton (Flight Test Manager). While a Hunter T.7 was chosen as chase plane for this flight, Hurricane PZ865 G-AMAU ('Last of the Many') was used for the transitional flight of the P.1127, due to its controllable speed range from 70 to 250 knots.

GOR.345 had, in the meantime, been replaced by NBMR-3, a scheme backed by NATO calling for a supersonic strike fighter. Hawker soon adapted the P.1127 design to qualify for such a specification, under the project number P.1154. Although the latter was never to achieve production status, experience gained in its planning contributed in no small way towards achieving a fully operational version of the P.1127. May of 1962 brought about an order for nine more aircraft (XS688-696). Through an agreement reached between Britain, the United States and West Germany, an evaluation squadron was established under the name of Tripartite Evaluation Squadron (TES) its CO being Wg Cdr D. Scrimgeour, RAF. This unit was based at West Raynham in 1964 and operated the Pegasus 5-powered version known as the 'Kestrel'. Operational flying began on 1st April 1965 and up to 30th November 1965 the trials generated a huge amount of data, including for the 938 take-offs and landings undertaken, which is a high figure considering the serviceability of the radical engine/airframe combination.

From Kestrel to Harrier

Another round of political axes fell on a number of aviation projects under development in January 1965, one of which was the P.1154. In compensation, ASR.384 was issued calling for a P.1127 development for use by the Royal Air Force (RAF). This was followed later that same year with an order for six pre-production aircraft, named 'Harrier' (XV276-281), the first of which flew in August 1966. Although resembling the Kestrel in many ways, the Harrier was virtually a new aircraft and its engineering can only be described as ingenious. For the first time ever, an aircraft was designed and built in such a way that every single panel in the fuselage, every wing and any of its panels, flap, aileron, wing tip, fin and all its panels, canopy, nose cone and every access door could be removed from one aircraft and bolted, screwed or riveted onto another without adjustment of any kind; and as if to emphasise this, access panels on early Harriers had clearly stamped on the inside the words 'Checked for Interchangeability'!

Powered by the Pegasus Mk.6, which was now providing 19,000 lb of thrust, the first four aircraft in this batch (XV276-279) were built with Kestrel-type fairing in front of the cold nozzles while the other two featured the later type of air intake fairings. All aircraft had the rectangular style intake and exhaust fairing on the forward engine bay doors for the twin 4Kva engine mounted alternators. These aircraft were finished in gloss polyurethane Dark Green/Dark Sea Grey/Light Aircraft Grey and carried 36" diameter red/white/blue roundels on upper and lower surfaces of the wings together with a 24" red/white/blue roundel on the intake sides (centred on No.5 auxiliary intake door) and fin flashes in the same colours. Serials were in standard 8" black characters on the rear fuselage, repeated below the wings in 20" high characters.

The pre-production run was followed by an initial batch of Harrier GR Mk.1s to full operational specification, made up of two batches. The first consisted of serial XV738-762, all of which were similarly finished to the first six aircraft described above. XV742 flew for a while with civil registration G-VSTO for a sales mission to Switzerland. This was followed by a second batch (XV776-810) but this time there was a change of markings believed to have begun with XV795. Air Staff policy had changed and lower visibility national markings were now required. These consisted of 24" diameter red/blue roundels on the intake sides while those above the wings – in the same colours – were reduced from 36" diameter to 30" and officially moved outboard by some two inches so that the outer edge of the red disc abutted against the outer edge of the Aileron Power Control Unit (PCU) access panel. Fin flashes were also changed to red/blue while roundels beneath the wings remained as before. XV743 crashed prior to delivery to the RAF and was replaced by XW630.

A second production batch of Harrier GR Mk.1s consisted of XW754-770. Due to a possible conflict of identification between XW754-762 with part of the first production batch (XV754-762) the former were re-serialled XW916-924.

A Harrier Conversion Team (HCT) was formed on 1 January 1969, led by Sqdn Ldr R.H.B. Le Brocq, spending the first three months with Hawker Siddeley at Dunsfold. Following the HCT to Wittering on 1 April, the first pair of GR Mk.1s arrived on 17 and 18 May with the first conversion course for No. 1(F) Squadron

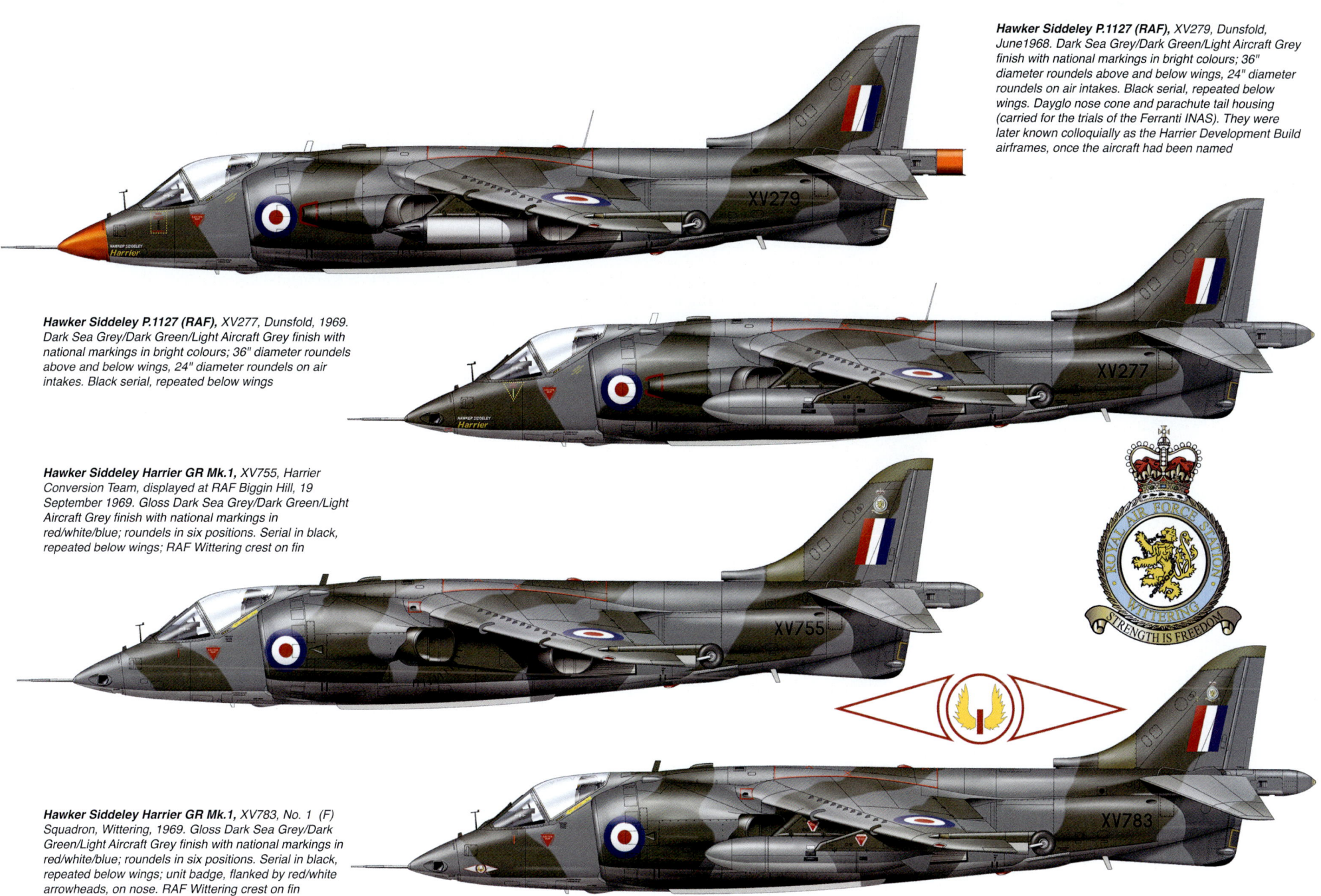

Hawker Siddeley P.1127 (RAF), XV279, Dunsfold, June 1968. Dark Sea Grey/Dark Green/Light Aircraft Grey finish with national markings in bright colours; 36" diameter roundels above and below wings, 24" diameter roundels on air intakes. Black serial, repeated below wings. Dayglo nose cone and parachute tail housing (carried for the trials of the Ferranti INAS). They were later known colloquially as the Harrier Development Build airframes, once the aircraft had been named

Hawker Siddeley P.1127 (RAF), XV277, Dunsfold, 1969. Dark Sea Grey/Dark Green/Light Aircraft Grey finish with national markings in bright colours; 36" diameter roundels above and below wings, 24" diameter roundels on air intakes. Black serial, repeated below wings

Hawker Siddeley Harrier GR Mk.1, XV755, Harrier Conversion Team, displayed at RAF Biggin Hill, 19 September 1969. Gloss Dark Sea Grey/Dark Green/Light Aircraft Grey finish with national markings in red/white/blue; roundels in six positions. Serial in black, repeated below wings; RAF Wittering crest on fin

Hawker Siddeley Harrier GR Mk.1, XV783, No. 1 (F) Squadron, Wittering, 1969. Gloss Dark Sea Grey/Dark Green/Light Aircraft Grey finish with national markings in red/white/blue; roundels in six positions. Serial in black, repeated below wings; unit badge, flanked by red/white arrowheads, on nose. RAF Wittering crest on fin

pilots beginning on 14 July, without the use of a simulator or a two-seat trainer; these were preceded by sorties whereby pilots became accustomed to VTOL techniques flying a Westland Whirlwind helicopter. On 1 April of the following year, the HCT became the Harrier Conversion Unit until another change in name that came on 1 October when it became officially known as No 233 Operational Conversion Unit (OCU).

Living up to its motto (Foremost in Everything) No 1 (F) Squadron RAF was given the task of proving the Harrier in operational service when it moved from West Raynham to Wittering in June of the same year. As can be expected of such a revolutionary machine, conversion was a long process and characterised by a number of problems. However, once these had been overcome the squadron championed the Harrier's unique qualities wherever it went. The unit's first overseas deployment was in March 1970 at Akrotiri (Cyprus), staging through Malta where yours truly gaped in utter amazement to see them landing and taking off in the length of a football pitch.

Second unit to be equipped with the Harrier was No IV (AC) Squadron RAF, which moved from Gutersloh, first to Wittering in March 1970 for conversion to the Harrier and then to Wildenrath where it received its first GR Mk.1s (XV779, 780) on 22 June. Second RAF Germany unit to pass onto the Harrier GR Mk.1 was No. 20, becoming officially operational on 1 December 1970.

Meanwhile Pegasus development and production had passed on to Rolls-Royce (following a Bristol-R.R. merger) from where the Pegasus Mk.102 of 20,000 lb thrust appeared. These engines were retrofitted to all GR Mk.1s and with it came a change in designation to GR Mk.1A. XW916-924 were built as Mk.1As and finished on the production line in matt Dark Sea Grey/Dark Green/Light Aircraft Grey while other Harriers in service began to receive the same matt finish. Markings remained the same as those for the last batch of GR Mk.1s, described above. These aircraft were produced as GR Mk.1As, but powered by the Pegasus 103 (21,000 lb thrust) but still retaining the twin 4Kva alternators. Problems with Rotax 12Kva alternators planned for the Mk.103 meant that some Pegasus engines of this type were only partially upgraded to the required standard. Apart from upgrading Harriers already in the field, a fourth unit – No 3 (F) Squadron – was formed in January 1972 at Wildenrath on the GR Mk.1A thus completing the Wildenrath Wing of three squadrons.

Exports
No sooner than the first RAF squadron was established in 1969, the United States Marine Corps (USMC) showed considerable interest in the Harrier and managed to obtain procurement permission and funds. Designated AV-8A, the USMC version was practically identical to the GR.1 and apart from replacing aircraft in attack squadrons it also formed the basis for a new concept known as Sea Control Ship, a light 15,000 ton carrier equipped with Harriers and helicopters. For this purpose *USS Guam* was converted and operated in such a role between 1971 and 1973. Tests on other carriers, such as the 14 Harriers operating from *USS Franklin D. Roosevelt* in 1976 proved that the aircraft could operate in weather where other fixed wing aircraft could not.

The versatility of the jump jet allowed the USMC to operate the Harriers in the close support role from makeshift bases closer to the battlefield than those required for conventional aircraft. In air-to-air combat and at the hands of an experienced pilot, the Harrier's vectoring-in-forward-flight (VIFF) could outmanouevre such a formidable opponent as the F-4 Phantom. Success in operating the Harrier encouraged the USMC to push for further development of the type and by 1979 units were being supplied with the updated AV-8C which featured further improvement to the Harrier's S/VTOL capablities and remained in service until the arrival of the second generation jump jets in 1987.

The capability of the Harrier's operation from small carriers prompted interest in the type by Spain. Unfortunately long standing problems between Britain and Spain meant that such procurement was fraught with problems and delays until a round-about way was found when the Harriers arrived thanks to the intervention of the United States. One other point that threatened this deal was the question whether the Harrier could possibly operated from wooden decks. Such fears were dispelled when in November 1972 tests at sea confirmed that no major problems were encountered. Designated AV-8S 'Matador', the aircraft entered service with the Spanish Navy on the carrier *Dédalo* (ex *USS Cabot*) in 1976.

On purchasing second generation Harriers, the Spanish Navy sold seven single seat and two twin-seat examples to the Royal Thai Navy for emplyment on the carrier Charki Naruebet. However the use of these Matadors was problematic due to funding shortages, lack of spares and maintenance and within two years only a single example remained airworthy.

Space was always at a premium at RAF Luqa (Malta), as can be seen from the gaggle of aircraft on Park No. 4 in summer of 1973. XV779/Q from No. 20 Squadron taxies out for take-off after a training detachment at Malta in August of that year. Note the 330-gallon long range tanks fitted for its flight to RAFG Wildenrath, hence the Victor tankers behind (Photo: Richard J. Caruana)

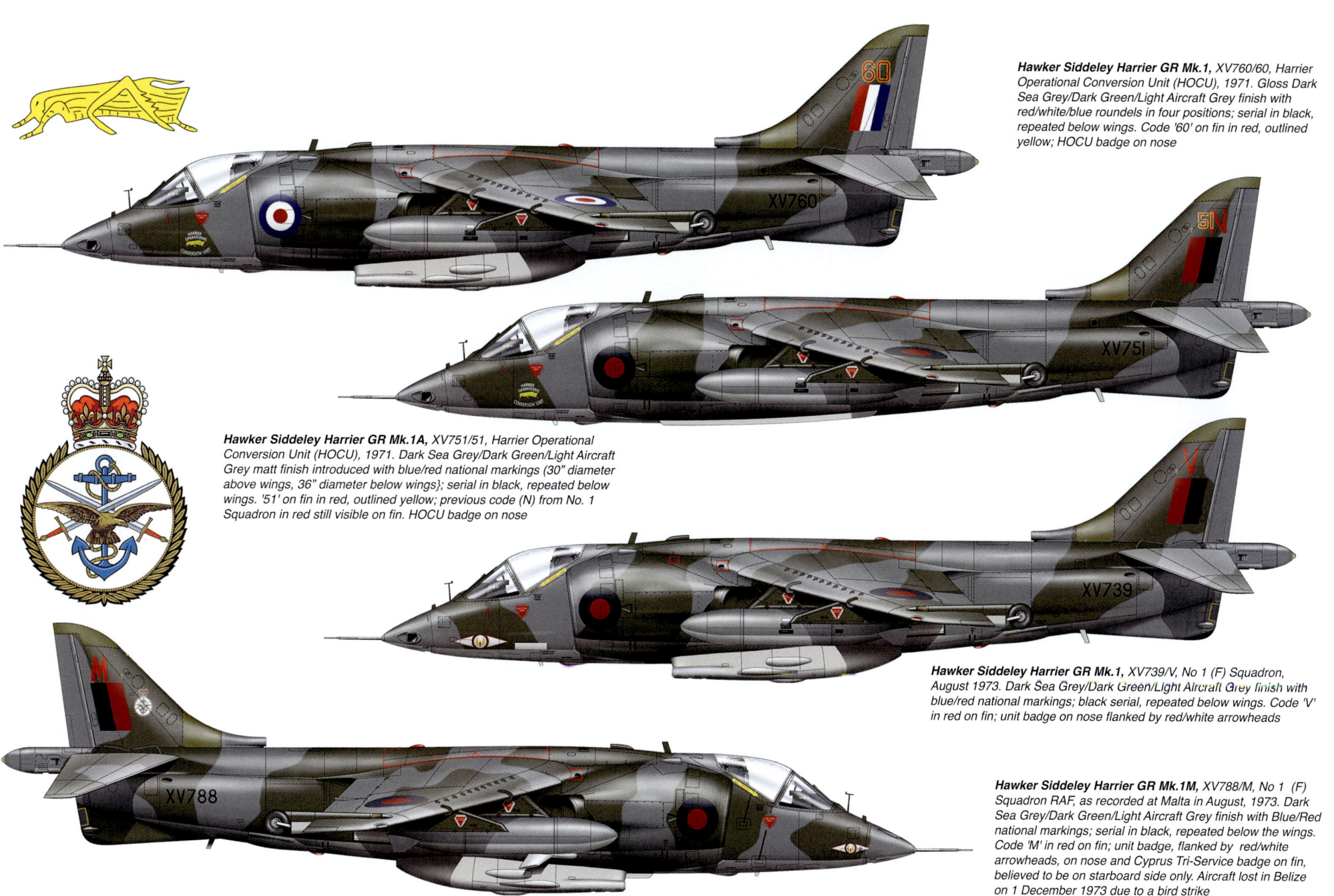

Hawker Siddeley Harrier GR Mk.1, XV760/60, Harrier Operational Conversion Unit (HOCU), 1971. Gloss Dark Sea Grey/Dark Green/Light Aircraft Grey finish with red/white/blue roundels in four positions; serial in black, repeated below wings. Code '60' on fin in red, outlined yellow; HOCU badge on nose

Hawker Siddeley Harrier GR Mk.1A, XV751/51, Harrier Operational Conversion Unit (HOCU), 1971. Dark Sea Grey/Dark Green/Light Aircraft Grey matt finish introduced with blue/red national markings (30" diameter above wings, 36" diameter below wings); serial in black, repeated below wings. '51' on fin in red, outlined yellow; previous code (N) from No. 1 Squadron in red still visible on fin. HOCU badge on nose

Hawker Siddeley Harrier GR Mk.1, XV739/V, No 1 (F) Squadron, August 1973. Dark Sea Grey/Dark Green/Light Aircraft Grey finish with blue/red national markings; black serial, repeated below wings. Code 'V' in red on fin; unit badge on nose flanked by red/white arrowheads

Hawker Siddeley Harrier GR Mk.1M, XV788/M, No 1 (F) Squadron RAF, as recorded at Malta in August, 1973. Dark Sea Grey/Dark Green/Light Aircraft Grey finish with Blue/Red national markings; serial in black, repeated below the wings. Code 'M' in red on fin; unit badge, flanked by red/white arrowheads, on nose and Cyprus Tri-Service badge on fin, believed to be on starboard side only. Aircraft lost in Belize on 1 December 1973 due to a bird strike

Four-View of Hawker Siddeley Harrier GR Mk.1, XV778/S, No 1 (F) Squadron, 1970. Gloss Dark Sea Grey/Dark Green/Light Aircraft Grey finish with red/white/blue roundels in six positions; serial in black, repeated below wings. Code 'S' in white on fin; unit badge on nose

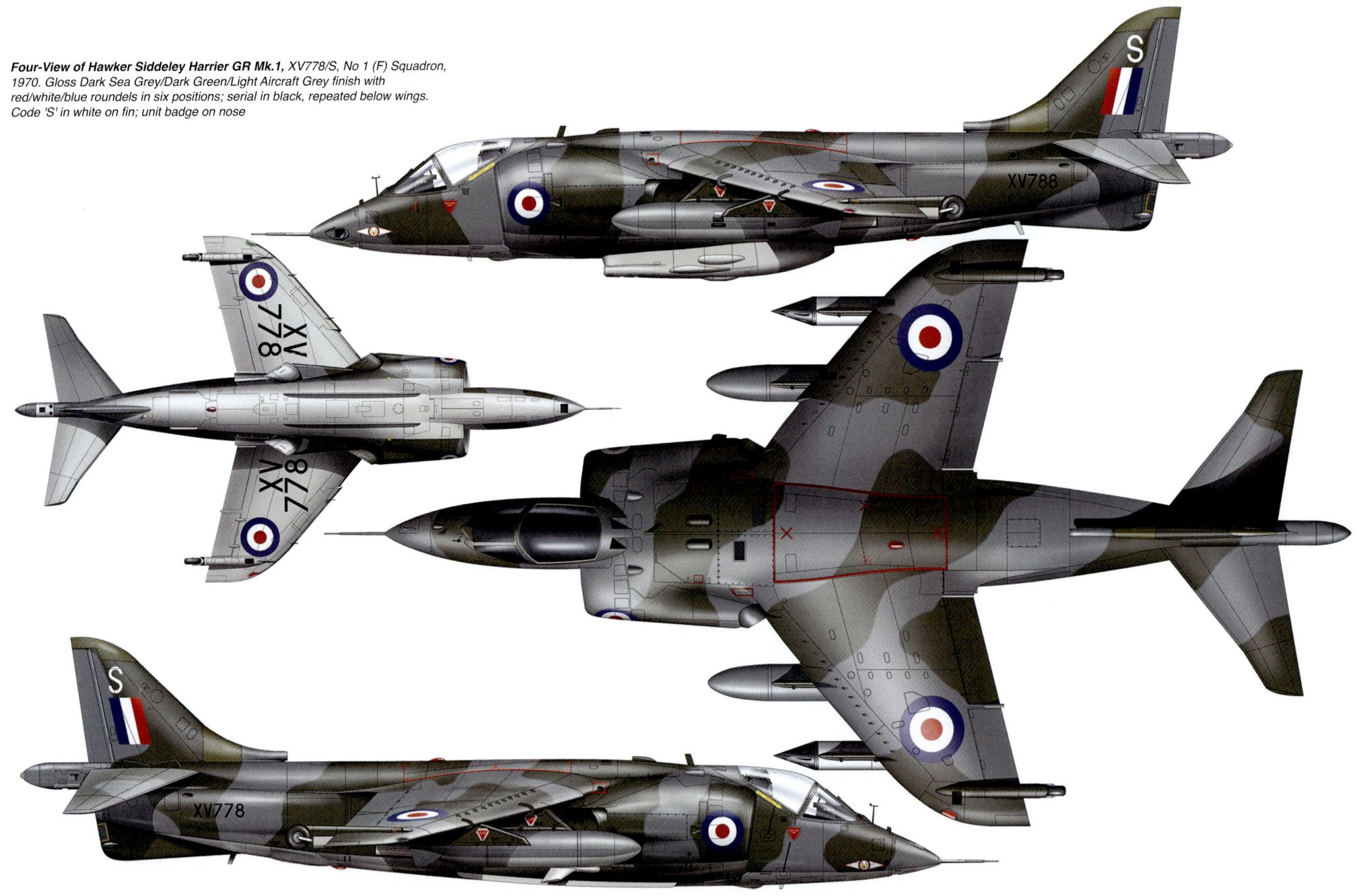

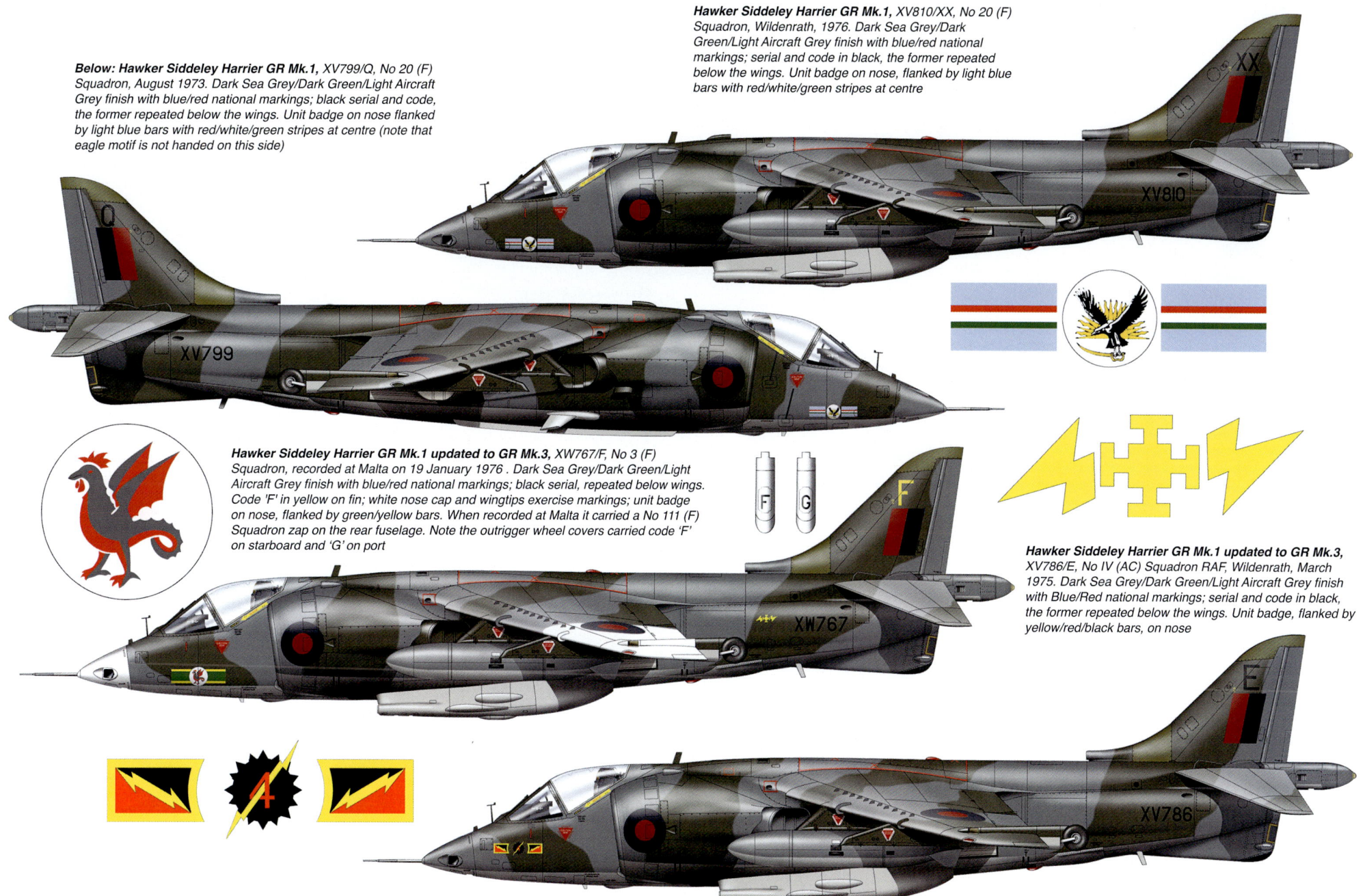

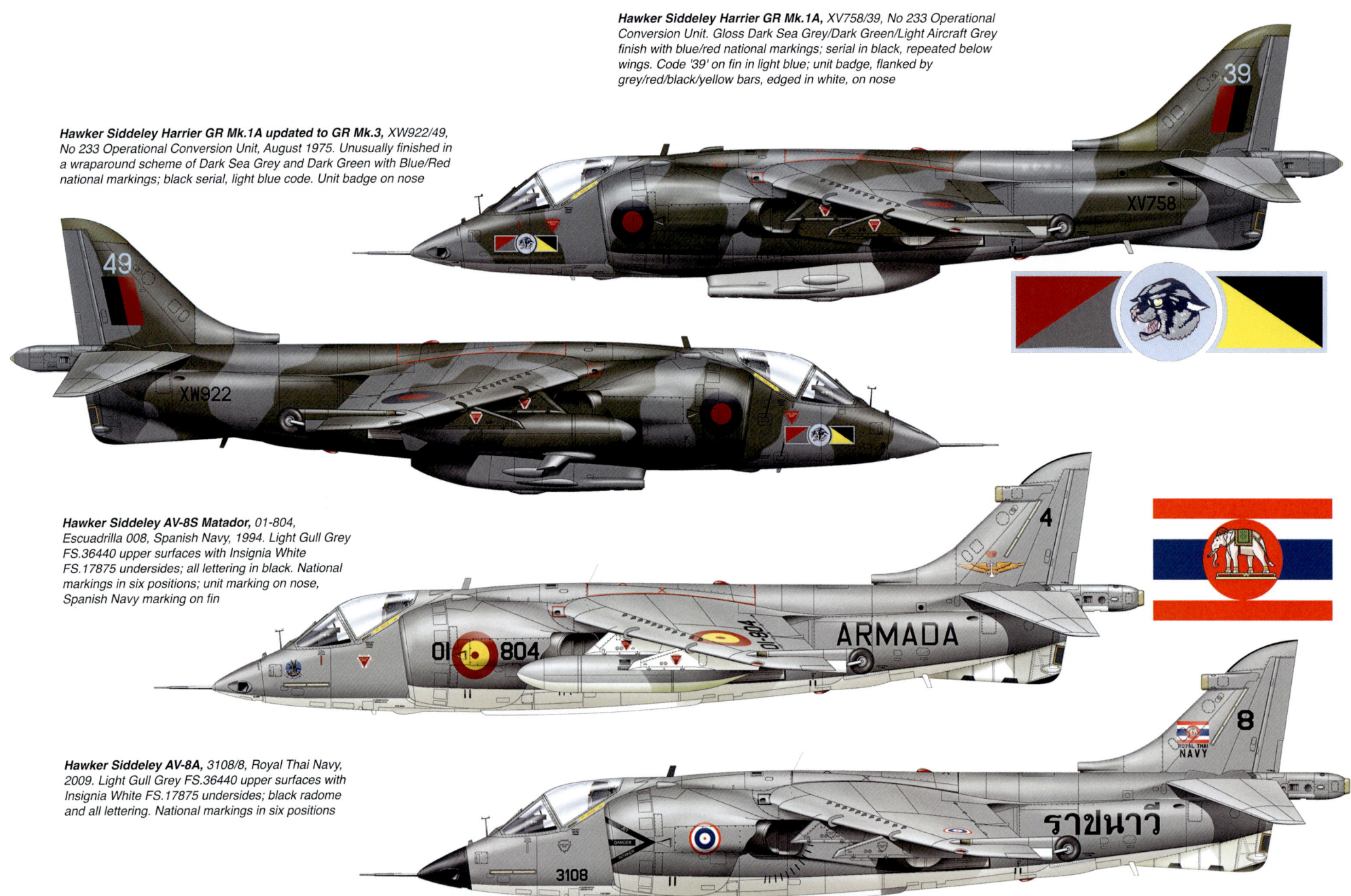

Hawker Siddeley Harrier GR Mk.1A, XV758/39, No 233 Operational Conversion Unit. Gloss Dark Sea Grey/Dark Green/Light Aircraft Grey finish with blue/red national markings; serial in black, repeated below wings. Code '39' on fin in light blue; unit badge, flanked by grey/red/black/yellow bars, edged in white, on nose

Hawker Siddeley Harrier GR Mk.1A updated to GR Mk.3, XW922/49, No 233 Operational Conversion Unit, August 1975. Unusually finished in a wraparound scheme of Dark Sea Grey and Dark Green with Blue/Red national markings; black serial, light blue code. Unit badge on nose

Hawker Siddeley AV-8S Matador, 01-804, Escuadrilla 008, Spanish Navy, 1994. Light Gull Grey FS.36440 upper surfaces with Insignia White FS.17875 undersides; all lettering in black. National markings in six positions; unit marking on nose, Spanish Navy marking on fin

Hawker Siddeley AV-8A, 3108/8, Royal Thai Navy, 2009. Light Gull Grey FS.36440 upper surfaces with Insignia White FS.17875 undersides; black radome and all lettering. National markings in six positions

Hawker Siddeley AV-8A Harrier, Bu.No.159251/3/WF, VMA-513 'The Flying Nightmares', Detachment 'A'. Dark Sea Grey/Dark Green/Light Aircraft Grey finish; standard national markings. Serial and 'Marines' on fin in black; all other lettering in mid-blue. Mid-blue rudder with white stars

Three Views of Hawker Siddeley AV-8A Harrier, Bu.No. 158703/703, USMC, during tests on USS Tarawa, 1981. Dark Sea Grey/Dark Green upper surfaces with Light Aircraft Grey undersides; International Orange fin and wingtips. Standard US national markings; lettering in black except '703' on nose which is white

GHIBLI AMX
The Hot Wind from the Desert

AERITALIA - AERMACCHI - EMBRAER

AMX Ghibli, MM.7149, 103° Gruppo/51° Stormo, Aeronautica Militare Italiana, in 50th Anniversary markings, 1993. Grigio Chairo FS.36280 overall with serial in black. Yellow flash on forward fuselage, outlined in black; 1943-1993 in black, outlined in yellow. Unit badge on fin. National markings on fuselage sides, above port and below starboard wings

AMX Ghibli, MM.7158/RS-12, Reparto Sperimentale Volo, Aeronautica Militare Italiana. Grigio Chiaro FS.36280 overall with all lettering in black. National markings on fuselage sides, above port and below starboard wings

AMX Ghibli, MM.7191/3-06, 132° Gruppo, 3° Stormo, Aeronautica Militare Italiana. Grigio Chiaro FS.36280 overall with all markings in black. National markings on fuselage sides, above port and below starboard wings

AMX Ghibli, MM.7125 (32-12), 13º Gruppo, 32º Stormo, Aeronautica Militare Italiana, 2001. Basic scheme of Grigio Chiaro FS 36280 overall with black trim to nose, underside of fuselage, wings and top of rear fuselage, blending in green trim towards the rear of the fuselage and vertical tail surfaces. Black/white sharkmouth motif, black gills. Unit badge on fin in white and black. Red heart, green four-leaf clover and black square on rudder. 10.000 hours of operations recorded on black underwing fuel tank in green

AMX Ghibli, MM7152/51•03, Indian '1', 103º Gruppo, 51º Stormo, Aeronautica Militare Italiana, 2003. Upper surfaces in Dark Sea Grey (FS.36118) and Dark Green (FS.34079) with undersides remaining in Grigio Chiaro FS.36280. Black/yellow trim to nose and vertical tail surfaces. Codes in white; high viz roundels in usual positions. Gruppo badge on air intakes, Stormo badge on fin

AMX Ghibli, MM.7133/51-30/33, 103º Gruppo, 51º Stormo, Aeronautica Militare Italiana, 2005. Grigio Chiaro FS.36280 overall with all markings in black, except 'Goose Bay 2005' emblem which is in red/white and black lettering. National markings on fuselage sides, above port and below starboard wings

AMX Ghibli, MM.7147/32-01, 32º Stormo Anniversary markings, Aeronautica Militare Italiana, 2006. Upper surfaces in a closely mottled scheme of dark green, reddish brown and sand; undersides in Grigio Chiaro FS.36280. Codes on nose are in black and red; lettering below cockpit in black. White cross on vertical tail surfaces with unit badge superimposed and a red '01' on top. National markings on fuselage sides, above port and below starboard wings. The scheme reflects that of Armando Boetto's S.79 of the 79ª Squadriglia, shot down in action over Gibraltar on 12 June 1940

AMX Ghibli, MM.7185/2-02, 14° Gruppo, 2°Stormo, Aeronautica Militare Italiana. Grigio Chiaro FS.36280 overall with all markings in black. National markings on fuselage sides, above port and below starboard wings. Note extended nose black area

AMX Ghibli, MM.7180/32-20, 32° Stormo, Aeronautica Militare Italiana, 2010. Grigio Chiaro FS.36280 overall with all lettering in black, except the 30,000 hour marking which is blue. Unit badge on fin in yellow and black. National markings above on fuselage sides, above port and below starboard wings

AMX-T Ghibli, MM.55048, 101° Gruppo, Aeronautica Militare Italiana, 2002. Basic scheme of Grigio Chiaro FS.36280 overall with section aft of cockpit overpainted in black, including above and below wings and tailplane. Medium blue snake with red flash and white/yellow sparks along the fuselage and fin. '10,000' in medium blue on underwing tank. Name on fin 'Centauro' in white. Crashed in September 2007

AMX-T Ghibli, MM.55037/32-64, 101° Gruppo, 32° Stormo, Aeronautica Militare Italiana, 2004. Grigio Chiaro FS.36280 overall with all lettering in black. Black flash above nose; black/white vertical tail surfaces with red flash superimposed. National markings on fuselage sides, above port and below starboard wings. Note different markings on starboard side of vertical tail surfaces

AMX A-1, 5502, 1º/16º GAv., Base Aérea de Santa Cruz (SC), Força Aérea Brasileira, 1989. Ocean Grey FS.35237 upper surfaces with Light Ghost Grey FS.35526 undersides; all lettering in black. National markings on fuselage sides and four wing positions. Unit badge on nose, repeated on air intakes

Above: AMX A-1, 5542, Esq Poker, 1º/10º G.Av., Base Aérea de Santa Maria (SM), Força Aérea Brasileira, 2003. Ocean Grey FS.35237 upper surfaces with Light Ghost Grey FS.35526 undersides; all lettering in black. National markings on fuselage sides and four wing positions. Unit badge on rudder in red

AMX A-1, 5520, 1º/16º GAv., Base Aérea de Santa Cruz (SC), Força Aérea Brasileira, 1998. Ocean Grey FS.35237 upper surfaces with Light Ghost Grey FS.35526 undersides; all lettering in black. National markings on fuselage sides and four wing positions. Unit badge on nose. Black nose, wing, fin and pylon leading edges

AMX A-1, 5500, 1º/16º GAv., Base Aérea de Santa Cruz (SC), Força Aérea Brasileira, 2006. Ocean Grey FS.35237 upper surfaces with Light Ghost Grey FS.35526 undersides; all lettering in black. National markings on fuselage sides and four wing positions. Stylised unit badge in black only on top of fin; 100th Anniversary of Santos Dumont's first flight badge on fin

AMX A-1, 5525, 1º/16º GAv., Base Aérea de Santa Cruz (SC), Força Aérea Brasileira, 1999. Ocean Grey FS.35237 upper surfaces with Light Ghost Grey FS.35526 undersides; all lettering in black. National markings on fuselage sides and four wing positions. Unit badge on nose with stylised version on top of fin. Black nose, wing, fin, front of external fuel tank and pylon leading edges. Brazilian flag applied on air intake for 'Red Flag 1999' exercise in the USA

Below: AMX A-1A, 5531, 3º/10º GAv, Base Aérea de Santa Maria (SM), Força Aérea Brasileira, 2008. Dark green FS.34092 upper surfaces with blue-grey FS.36176 undersides; national markings in same colours, in six positions. All lettering in black. Unit badge over a black horizontal band across vertical tail surfaces, outlined in white

AMX A-1A, 5506, 1º/16º GAv, Base Aérea de Santa Cruz (SC), Força Aérea Brasileira, 2008. Dark green FS.34092 upper surfaces with blue-grey FS.36176 undersides; national markings in same colours, in six positions. All lettering in black. Unit badge in black only on rudder; 20th Anniversary badge on fin

AMX A-1B, 5659, 1º/10º GAv, Base Aérea de Santa Maria (SM), Força Aérea Brasileira, 2005. Dark green FS.34092 upper surfaces with blue-grey FS.36176 undersides; national markings in same colours, in six positions. All lettering in black. Unit badge on rudder in red with black drop shadow

AMX A-1, 5530, 1º/10º GAv, Base Aérea de Santa Maria (SM), Força Aérea Brasileira. Dark green FS.34092 upper surfaces with blue-grey FS.36176 undersides; national markings in same colours, in six positions. All lettering in black. Unit badge in grey with black drop shadow on rudder

AMX A-1B, FAB 5657/Alpha 4, 3º/10º GAv, Força Aérea Brasileira, October 2005. Ocean Grey FS.35237 upper surfaces with Light Ghost Grey FS.35526 undersides; all lettering in black. National markings on fuselage sides and four wing positions. Unit badge in black on top of fin over a thin black band; 'alpha' 4 in black on nose

AMX A-1B, 5654/Beta-3, 3º/10º GAv, Força Aérea Brasileira, 2001. Experimental scheme in FS.34092 and FS.36176 upper surfaces; FS.36463 undersides; national markings in same colours, in six positions. All lettering in black. 'Beta 3' on nose in black within a black outlined rectangle

AMX A-1B, 5654, 3º/10º GAv, Força Aérea Brasileira. Dark green FS.34092 upper surfaces with blue-grey FS.36176 undersides; national markings in same colours, in six positions. All lettering in black. Unit badge on rudder in white over a black band with thin white top and bottom outlines. 30th Anniversary logo on fin